Response Journals Revisited

Maximizing learning through
reading, writing, viewing, discussing,
and thinking

LES PARSONS

Stenhouse Publishers
PORTLAND, MAINE

Pembroke Publishers Limited
MARKHAM, ONTARIO

To Susan Clifton,

whose expertise and insights

infuse these pages

© **2001 Pembroke Publishers**
538 Hood Road
Markham, Ontario, Canada L3R 3K9
www.pembrokepublishers.com

Published in the U.S. by Stenhouse Publishers
477 Congress Street
Portland, ME 04101
ISBN 1-57110-345-7
www.stenhouse.com

We acknowledge the financial support of the Government of Canada through th Book Publishing Industry Development Program (BPIDP) for our publishin activities.

National Library of Canada Cataloguing in Publication Data

Parsons, Les, 1943-
    Response journals revisited: maximizing learning through
reading, writing, viewing, discussing, and thinking

Includes index.
ISBN 1-55138-131-1

    1. School children — Diaries. 2. Creative writing (Middle school)
3. Reading (Middle School). I. Title.

LB1631.P37 2001   372.6   C2001-901390-6

Editor: Kate Revington
Cover Design: John Zehethofer
Cover Photo: Ajay Photographics
Typesetting: Jay Tee Graphics Ltd.

Printed and bound in Canada
9 8 7 6 5 4 3 2 1

Contents

Preface

It's time to revisit journal writing. The original confusion surrounding the introduction of journals has only grown worse over the years, to the extent that many teachers now equate journals with learning logs or language arts or English notebooks. Journals are neither, as this updated, expanded, and revised handbook on journal writing emphatically indicates.

Response Journals Revisited dispels all confusion by explaining, step by step, what response journals are, why and how they're used, the skills they're meant to develop, and how journals are formatively and summatively evaluated.

It's also time to put the *response* back into response journals. Response theory lies at the heart of this multifaceted learning/teaching strategy. Containing a comprehensive catalogue of guidelines and rubrics for students and teachers, numerous sample student responses, as well as extensive background information, *Response Journals Revisited* clarifies how personal response can expand, deepen, and renew reading and literature programs, media literacy studies, and cooperative learning strategies.

In spite of the widespread emphasis on journal writing across the curriculum, teachers, for the most part, have not had the grounding they need to know why and how to implement the strategy. For experienced teachers who wonder what all the fuss is about or for teachers new to the profession, it's time to take a fresh look at response journals.

1

What's so good about response journals?

When educational innovations become institutionalized, fossilization often sets in. Function and form become interchangeable.

Look at what has happened to writing folders, for example. They were first introduced to mirror and facilitate a process-oriented approach to writing and to create a unique window into an individual's growth in writing over time. Regrettably, the use of folders was far easier to implement than a true process orientation to writing. As many teachers discovered, over the course of decades the form outlasted the function. Whatever the potential of the writing folder system, in actual practice, it frequently breaks down. Unless a *genuine* process approach to writing guides and directs the process, the folders often degenerate into storage compartments for loose bits of paper from anywhere and everywhere.

Is the use of journals adopted out of obligation or conviction?

As for journals, they are in danger of succumbing to a similar fate.

The popularity of journal writing has been a mixed blessing. First introduced into language arts and English programs, they are also promoted for subject areas ranging from physical education to mathematics. While the use of response journals has been encouraged, even extolled, teachers have been left, by and large, to puzzle out for themselves the why's and how's of implementation.

Teachers have cause to wonder about the value of journals. They often report that their students dislike writing regularly in a journal, that their entries tend to be repetitive in topic, treatment, and detail, and that they write as little as possible. Many of these problems stem from confusion over what journals really are, how they should be used and evaluated, and where journal writing fits in the total language program.

Unless journal writing is rooted in conviction, the practice endures like an unwanted guest. Everyone involved just goes through the motions, unable to find satisfaction or closure. In too many cases, either the teacher is burdened with the task of coming up with a daily journal topic or students have free choice to write about whatever they like. In either scenario, entries entail a few perfunctory sentences and tend to degenerate into simple narratives detailing what the students did the night before, what they had for breakfast, or what rock groups they like best.

Journal writing often turns into a kind of enforced diary-keeping, disliked by everyone involved. While some teachers are able to adapt writing in journals to fill specific needs in their programs, many are left wondering why so much precious classroom time is devoted to what seems on the surface to be a limited strategy.

Is it any wonder that many teachers include journal writing in their programs out of a sense of obligation rather than conviction?

Check for yourself whether it's time to reassess, redirect, and reinvigorate the use of journals in your classroom. It's definitely time, if you hear *yourself* saying . . .

"I don't have time to correct a class set of journals."
"My students have done journals for so many years before they get to me that they find journal writing boring."
"I have to tell my students every day what to write about and how much to write."
"What should I do if someone really doesn't have anything to say about a particular topic?"
"How are you supposed to mark journals?"
"What's the point of letting them choose their own topics if all they want to write about is wrestling?"

It's definitely time, if you're tired of hearing your *students* say . . .

"We did journals last year. Why do we have to do them again?"
"What should I write about?"
"What if I don't have anything to say about that?"
"I wrote about that last year. Can I say the same things?"
"Does spelling count?"
"How long does it have to be?"
"Does this count on report cards?"
"Can I write about wrestling?"

Depending on how they're implemented, response journals turn into another bandwagon to abandon — or become the key that illuminates and revitalizes learning across the curriculum. It's time to reassess what response journals are, what they are supposed to do, and how they should be implemented. It's time to get back to the basics with response journals.

Just what is a response journal?

Response journals combine the most useful aspects of learning logs and work diaries with contemporary response theory. They thereby fill the need for a flexible and multidimensional learning/teaching tool. Since evaluation directs and supports the learning, formative and summative evaluation (see Chapter 6) are integral components of this approach.

Although response journals are often confused with other approaches, they are different from personal diaries, writers' journals, and work diaries, learning logs, or subject-specific logs. You may find the following descriptions helpful:

- *Personal diary:* daily, spontaneous private writing; teachers do not read it unless given permission by the student; such writing grew out of the practice of daily "free" writing (the belief that writing for the sake of writing was beneficial); adopted by English/language arts teachers to develop the habit of daily writing
- *Writer's journal:* carried and maintained by choice, a source book for writing containing random jottings made at home or school; its use grew out of the writer's workshop or writing-as-process approach to creative writing; valued as a method of extracting first-draft material from everyday life
- *Learning logs/Work diaries:* day-to-day written records of what is done in a particular subject area and what and how students are learning; commonly used when students are working independently for extended periods, such as on projects
- *Subject-specific journals*: similar to a log or work diary, but including additional information about how students feel about what they're doing, as well as a formative self-evaluation component; these grew out of the recognition of the importance of metacognition in learning, but without the reliance on personal response (an explanation of both terms follows these descriptions); can be applied to any unit of study in any subject area
- *Response journal*: a notebook, folder, section of a binder, or electronic file in which students record their personal reactions to, questions about, and reflections on what they read, view, write, represent, observe, listen to, discuss, do, and think and how they go about reading, viewing, writing, representing, observing, listening, discussing, or doing; first used extensively in English/language arts programs; can be adapted to any unit of study in any subject area

Unlike other types of journals, the concept of personal response lies at the heart of response journals. In reading, for example, since comprehension springs from the mind as opposed to the page, students are asked to make connections and build bridges between their own reading and the previous vicarious and real experiences that might have influenced their interpretation of what they've read. (See Chapter 3 for a comprehensive examination of personal response in reading and literature.)

Through personal response, learning is personalized, deepened, and extended, and higher-level thinking processes are regularly addressed. Personal response is, in fact, ideally suited to the vagaries and "messiness" of many higher-level thinking skills, from the unpredictability of the individual paths leading to insight to the emotional, subjective content of understanding and memory.

Why learn through personal response?

Brain research supports this complex model of learning. Current research asserts that intuition, holistic imaging, and synthesis, supposedly right-hemispheric functions, can be accomplished by either of the brain's spheres. Some educators have previously theorized that since the left brain controls speech and most

9

language functions and the right brain controls visual-spatial skills, by diagnosing a child's tendencies towards left- or right-brain use, teachers could teach to the favored function.

Since the brain is a profoundly complex, integrated, and interconnected entity, such simplistic or one-dimensional approaches to learning fail to address the bewildering array of potential connections it might make in its search for meaning. The image of a butterfly flexing its wings in Brazil and creating a chain of events that results in the creation of thunderclouds in Nova Scotia hints at the myriad, often obscure linkages that result in the brain's understanding of a specific event.

Since a healthy brain is a multifaceted, interconnected whole, teachers need to address its intrinsic mode of learning. For this reason, learning is optimized in a language-rich, varied, and stimulating environment that emphasizes problem-solving in a holistic and integrated manner.

Through journal writing, students are constantly testing their understanding of reality by clarifying, discovering, assessing, reflecting on, resolving, and refining what they really think and feel about experience. Personal response encourages students to problem-solve in a self-directed, specific, and meaningful manner.

Response journals also reflect both the integrated nature of language use and the importance of a process orientation in a classroom setting. As students learn through language, they may need to incorporate aspects of listening, speaking, reading, writing, and viewing to achieve their purposes. A single writing task, for example, may engage a student in a range of discussion, writing, and reading activities in a recursive and blended manner. Response journals are flexible enough to accommodate such a complex, integrated process.

Personal response, as well, recognizes that emotions play a key role in learning. While educators have long accepted the axiom that affective and cognitive behaviors are two sides of the same coin, they still need to recognize the inseparable and interdependent nature of that relationship. To strip content of its emotional connotations and denotations would impede learning. Our emotions are instrumental in shaping our understanding of reality. The visible tip of an underlying foundation of values and attitudes, our emotions influence how we prioritize the elements of any experience and how we feel about the experience itself.

No two people experience the same event in exactly the same way. Our emotions color and filter everything we see, hear, taste, touch, and smell. An animal rights activist and a lifelong aficionado, for example, would construct dramatically different versions of the same bullfight. With a class of thirty students watching a film and registering a range of reactions from enthralled joy to total disinterest, the subjective nature of learning is compellingly under-scored. For all students, the path to an objective appreciation of the intellectual content of a learning experience begins with an investigation into an individual's emotional response.

As well, memories are always being created and recreated in a dynamic process linked to emotion. From the moment we experience something, our memories are broken down into fragments that are stored in many places all over the brain. The memory of a rose isn't found in any one place in the cerebrum; instead, it is created anew from subunits of sensation based on color, shape, and smell every time a person thinks of a rose. The "mind's eye" that records reality like a videotape recorder does not exist. Instead, the mind subjectively recreates from experience a constantly evolving film that we call our memories.

Rather than being separated from their past and present experiences, students need to use those contexts as entry points into new experiences and new discoveries. They can then extend the search for meaning by exploring all the connections, especially emotional, that an experience evokes.

What brain research is telling educators is that the brain will learn, especially when students are actively involved in the learning process and taking responsibility for and making many of the decisions related to their own learning.

Schools have a long way to go in this regard, though. Many teachers devote much of their time to assigning and marking work and relatively little time to activities related to explaining and modelling thinking processes. The most used reading activities, for instance, involve students in recalling, copying, and demonstrating facts, in other words, proving that they have read what they were supposed to read. The least used reading activities call upon students to summarize or synthesize material or analyze an author's style.

Students are seldom asked to reflect thoughtfully on the material they read. Reflective language, nonetheless, ignites and illuminates all learning through a process that educational jargon terms *metacognition*. Metacognition refers to the ability to consciously reflect on and talk about thinking; specifically, learners begin to focus on their patterns of thought and become aware of how and, eventually, why they process experience the specific way they do. This ability is enhanced by developmental factors and encouraged by reflective practices, such as personal response.

The following student muses on maturity and her own thought processes in the course of reflecting on her previous year's approach to journal writing. Notice that she discovers for herself that she does indeed think through writing and that her analysis of literature often becomes another pathway into an examination of reality.

Throughout the book, you will find a number of sample student responses, such as this one, illustrating the many applications of response journals. Spelling errors in the student responses have been corrected, but other stylistic features of student writing remain as they appeared in the original copy.

Response to "growing up,"
Feb.14

I think that growing up is important in life because if you stay the same person your whole life you miss out on different things. I was reading through my old journals from grade 7 yesterday and I found out things that made me laugh.

I read my first response and it was a sentence long. I told nothing about the book. I didn't even state my opinion. Then I read another one where I did at least say why I liked or disliked the book and what the author could have done to make it better.

Then I started reading the responses I did in grade 8. I found them to be more insightful and more thoughtful than my grade 7 responses. Not only did I tell a little bit about the story and state my opinion about that passage, I also go and sometimes give my opinion on how it relates to the real world. People should give their opinions more. Maybe then the world would be a better place.

When I finish my responses they often have nothing to do with the beginning. But as you read the response, you see how it flows because, when I write, my next ideas are triggered by what I had previously written. So all my responses are linked in idea and they are related in some way.

Rebecca (age 13)

Learning is an active, creative process. Most definitions of ideal learners emphasize that they are independent, self-motivated individuals who have the ability to find and solve their own problems. This kind of empowerment can only come through the acquisition of a complex set of sophisticated, metacognitive skills.

By definition, effective learners are objectively and profoundly aware of their own learning processes. Personal response helps students grow into independent, confident learners.

The purpose of responding is reflection

The purpose for a piece of writing determines whether or not that writing enters the revising/editing cycle of the writing process or is left in rough form. Writing and thinking are so closely linked that, for many people, they're interdependent. When language is being used for thinking, editing can actually destroy the process.

The purpose for writing in a response journal is *reflection*, not publishing. Since language is for thinking as well as for communicating, when we are learning through language, that use of language can be hesitant, tentative, halting, repetitive, and recursive. The goal is understanding.

The use of response journals and learning logs acknowledges how essential a student's personal language is in learning. If surface errors in spelling and grammar or mode of expression were "marked" in logs and journals, the benefits deriving from their use would be negated. If fluency became a criterion, the informal, everyday, repetitive, and recursive language of personal thought would dry up and the problem-solving processes would short-circuit.

The issue of whether or not to correct errors is pivotal to successful implementation. Since personal response directs students to examine the crucial link between how and what they learn, evaluation must be based on *learning* criteria rather than on fluency criteria. (Please see Chapter 6, Evaluating Response Journals, for a comprehensive explanation of how to evaluate response journals.)

Ideally, personal response acts first as a mirror, enabling individuals to recognize what they're thinking and the patterns created by that process; in the subsequent, reflective stage, the responses then form a window into the nature of these thoughts, establishing how and why individuals learn.

The series of responses that follows reveals one student's journey into personal response.

Before discovering William Bell's historical novel, *The Forbidden City*, which is set in China during the Tiananmen Square uprising, the student had difficulty finding books that interested him. He usually chose simple narratives. In one instance, he read a book about Eric the Red only because his own name was Eric. His responses were mainly brief, perfunctory descriptions of plot.

As he works his way through *The Forbidden City*, however, the student becomes emotionally involved, propelled by his response to the plot into an inflamed cognitive awareness. His journey begins slowly and, at first, without comment, as he merely records what and how much he is reading each day. From a terse beginning (he made no responses on January 8 and 9, recording only that he had read 45 pages at home), his reflections gradually build to an unforgettable climax.

Responses to *The Forbidden City*

Pages 46–52 (at home), Jan. 10	*I've never been in Beijing before, but I think that's what it looks like.*
Pages 53–89 (at home), Jan. 11	*Every time I read, I'm waiting for that one day that the author is making me wait for when the army arrives and Alex tries to escape.*
Pages 90–111 (at home), Jan. 12	*I really like the part where Alex talks Chinese and the "Ma" thing. I wonder if the author had learned Chinese before writing this book. The story is starting to get sort of exciting as Alex learns more about the government of China which I hate AND CAN'T DO ANYTHING ABOUT! IT MAKES ME MAD!*
Pages 112–44 (at school), Jan. 17	*The part about the demonstration is the beginning of HELL. I am scared, scared of when the army will come and kill all the innocent people. Don't you get angry? I think if this book is shipped to China, whoever buys the book will get executed.*
Pages 145–81 (at home), Jan. 20	*RUN, ALEX! RUN! Lao Xu is dead. Now I am angry. Lao Xu didn't even say a thing or do a thing. The girl just shot him! I mean what kind of a country is this? This country is rubbish! I feel ashamed to belong to this country.*
Pages 182–274 (at school), Jan. 25	*The last part about how he got on the bike and pretended to be Chinese is really exciting. Now I am mad again, just like Alex at the end. The girl got killed! I couldn't believe it. She would be a real hero to me if this story happened in real life and I think something similar really did happen in China. When will it change? The head of China and the government are able to do what they do only because of the suffering of the real treasure of China, the ordinary people.*
	I think it would be really great if they make this book into a movie, but that would be impossible because the stupid, cruel, and old Chinese government will not let it happen.
	When I was a boy, I said that when I grew up I would be the head of China and make it a free country. But I gave up my dream. I lost hope for my country.

Eric (age 13)

Concerns That Teachers Express About Journal Use

Implementing any kind of educational innovation can be a confusing and troublesome process. The questions and answers below address some common concerns that many teachers have about the place and use of response journals in their programs.

Q. I'm already using journals and my students don't like them. Why should I use them even more?

A. Response journals are qualitatively different from other types of journals, from the ways in which they're used to how entries are evaluated. Many

13

students have experienced more limited and confining approaches to journal writing and are understandably bored with the whole idea. Response journals, on the other hand, could form the core of your language arts or English program. As you move through the chapters in this book, notice how many listening, speaking, reading, writing, and viewing functions are well served by the personal response process.

Q. If students can write whatever they want, what's to keep them from filling pages with mindless rambling?
A. Direction from the teacher is not only acceptable in personal response, but necessary. Some teachers have expressed concern about interfering with the learning process or narrowing the scope by assigning a specific response to the class as a whole or by criticizing either the content or the form of an entry. On the contrary, intervention is part of the process.

Teachers need to guide students through to an awareness that meaningful reflection is the goal, not simply writing responses. They need to illustrate for students how specific responses can be strengthened to achieve that end. They need to discuss with their students how frequently and thoughtfully students are responding, as well as dealing with the form those responses are taking. On occasion, teachers even need to assign specific topics for students to consider.

Q. How often should I have my students write in their journals?
A. Response journals have so many applications that overuse is a common pitfall. Responding intensely every day is exhausting and blunts enthusiasm. As a general rule, depending on the grade level and the group, requiring a response every second or third day sets a minimum standard and seems to work best. By all means, encourage students to respond whenever they want to about anything that moves or intrigues them. Try, too, to vary the nature of their mandatory responses; if students responded to their reading one day, they might find exploring media or the dynamics of a group discussion more compelling for the next period.

Q. Where do I find the time to use response journals?
A. Using response journals will *save* you time. As an all-purpose learning/teaching tool, a response journal will allow you to consolidate in one place a variety of your language arts or English components. This one comprehensive file will make it easier for you to track, observe, and evaluate student language progress.

Q. How can you mark journals if you aren't even supposed to correct them?
A. Although it's true that response journals should not be marked for mechanical accuracy or stylistic features, if used properly, they can form the basis on which you evaluate a student's language progress, summatively as well as formatively. The key is focusing on learning criteria. (See Chapter 6.)

Q. How can students improve their writing if you don't point out their errors?
A. The revising/editing cycle of your writing-as-process program will help your students with the form of their writing. The response journal will allow students to shape, explore, clarify, and develop their thinking in their own spontaneous language. If students choose to use one of their responses as first-draft material for an essay, for example, then you would expect them to revise and edit the

14

material appropriately. In your total program, criteria are established and skills are taught.

Q. When can I find the time to write to every student?
A. Although you need to read the journals on a regular basis, you shouldn't be writing to every student every time you do. A brief, individual conference may be necessary for some students. If you need to offer written comments or suggestions to selected students, use the small, Post-it note pads. Some teachers establish a marking code to let students know in a simple, direct way the general quality of their responses. (Again, please see Chapter 6 for more details.)

Q. When I hand out sheets of instructions or guiding questions, my students just lose them. How can I get them to organize their journal work and keep it all together?
A. Some teachers use a folder, duotang, or a section of the student binder as the physical equivalent of a journal. In these cases, filing is simplified. When a notebook is used, insist that students fold and glue or staple vital loose-leaf sheets. For electronic files, instructions and other kinds of direction are easily transferred to the individual student files from a server.

2

Getting started with response journals

Response journals are designed to support rather than supplant existing programs. Since the technique is versatile and malleable, teachers can tailor how they use response journals to match their students' needs and the approach to instruction already in place.

Teachers should first sort through the many applications and decide which ones they would like to implement. Even if students have used response journals in the past, they may not have used them for the purposes listed below. Response journals can serve a variety of valuable functions:

- Students can use them to explore and reflect on such experiences as independent reading, a film or television program, a readaloud, and a small-group discussion.
- The journals provide a way for learning to be integrated across the curriculum.
- They serve as a simple tracking device to record what and how much has been read or to note individual perspectives on the discussion dynamics of a group.
- They provide a place to record observations and questions prior to a reading conference as well as comments and suggestions derived from the conference.
- Individual students can "dialogue" in written form with the teacher or their peers.
- The journals act as a reference file (e.g., a reading portfolio) to help both student and teacher monitor individual development and progress for both formative and summative evaluation purposes.
- They become source books of ideas, thoughts, opinions, and first drafts.

What do students know about response journals?

The next step in implementing response journals is finding out what students already know about them. Whatever the grade level, students come to a new classroom with pre-set attitudes toward and a number of proven strategies for dealing with the language demands already made upon them. Students are never blank slates. Teachers can gain much useful information by going straight to the source — the students themselves.

Given the multitude of practices falling under the umbrella term *journals*, teachers need to know right from the start what students understand the term to mean. Quickly getting to know what kind of experiences students have had with journals is crucial. A simple questionnaire can serve several functions. A questionnaire takes stock of a situation in a direct, objective manner and also provides a backdrop against which goals can be established, objectives defined, and action plans drawn up.

The sample student questionnaire on page 18 asks students questions about their past classroom experiences with journal writing. The object is to gather data, however, not to pry into the workings of previous classrooms. Such information helps the teacher decide how various concepts or routines involving response journals should be introduced and paced with specific groups of students.

Looking at the results of the questionnaire will give teachers some sense of what the term *journal* means to students and the kinds of journal writing they've already experienced. Teachers can then predict the aspects of implementation that will probably go smoothly and those that will require more explanation and monitoring. Depending on how students feel about their prior journal experiences, teachers may have to "sell" them on the value of response journals.

What do you want students to know about response journal writing?

In any case, when journals are introduced, students need to know in detail the expectations, requirements, and routines associated with response journals. A general introduction is useful to get them started.

The student guideline, "How to Use Response Journals," can be used as is or adapted and modified to suit a particular program. It appears on page 19.

Student Questionnaire

Experiences with Journal Writing

Please think about the most recent year in which journal writing formed some part of your school program to help you complete this questionnaire.

In what subjects did you keep a journal?(Please check as many as required.)

❑ Language Arts/English   ❑ History/Geography   ❑ Science   ❑ Math   ❑ Other

For the rest of the questions, please answer *only* for the journal you kept in your Language Arts/English program.

1. How often did you write in your journal? (Please check *one*.)

❑ Almost every day   ❑ 2–3 times per week   ❑ Once a week   ❑ Less than once a week

2. How much did you usually write each time?(Please check *one*.)

❑ Less than 1/2 page   ❑ 1/2–1 page   ❑ More than 1 page

3. How often did you receive a mark for your journal? (Please check *one*.)

❑ Almost every response   ❑ Every 1–2 weeks   ❑ Every 3–6 weeks   ❑ Every term

4. What kinds of topics did you write about?(Please check *one* box for each topic.)

• my reading	❑ Never	❑ Sometimes	❑ Often
• readalouds	❑ Never	❑ Sometimes	❑ Often
• videos/TV/movies	❑ Never	❑ Sometimes	❑ Often
• classroom activities	❑ Never	❑ Sometimes	❑ Often
• discussions	❑ Never	❑ Sometimes	❑ Often
• my own life	❑ Never	❑ Sometimes	❑ Often

5. How often did you choose what you wanted to write about? (Please check *one*.)

❑ Never   ❑ Sometimes   ❑ Often   ❑ Always

6. How often did the teacher assign a topic to write about? (Please check *one*.)

❑ Never   ❑ Sometimes   ❑ Often   ❑ Always

7. Was your journal marked for spelling and usage errors? (Please check *one*.)

❑ Yes   ❑ No

8. How often did you enjoy writing in a journal?(Please check *one*.)

❑ Never   ❑ Sometimes   ❑ Often   ❑ Always

Student Guideline

How to Use Response Journals

Many of you have written regularly in some kind of journal before coming to this class; however, the practice of journal writing varies widely. To benefit fully from this program, you need to understand, specifically, how journals will be handled in this class and how your work will be evaluated. A few general guidelines follow:

- You won't be required to respond in your journal every day, but your teacher will set the standard for a minimum number of responses. Feel free to make more responses whenever an issue, topic, or question interests, moves, intrigues, or puzzles you. Thoughtful additions to the minimum standard will be rewarded when your journal entries are evaluated.
- The work in your journal will *not* be corrected for spelling, usage, or grammatical errors. Your responses *will* be evaluated regularly, however, and the marks will be used for reporting purposes. Your teacher will inform you later about how, when, and on what basis your journal entries will be judged.
- When making handwritten entries, remember that both you and your teacher must be able to read them easily. Legibility is essential.
- From time to time, your teacher will supply you with printed instructions, such as this introductory guideline. This guideline and all other handouts related to journal writing should be retained as part of your journal. If you're using a notebook as a journal, please fold and glue or staple essential loose-leaf sheets into it.
- Since your journal serves as a reading portfolio, you and your teacher need to examine your progress over time. Whenever you read school-related material, record in your journal the title of the book you're reading, the page at which you started that day, and the page at which you finished. Please date each entry and indicate where the reading took place. For example:

April 29, The Dear One, pg. 26–42 (home)

If the reading isn't recorded, it can't be counted when your journal is evaluated.
- In the back of your journal, please keep a running inventory of the reading you complete. Your evolving inventory should look something like this:

Student Reading Inventory

Date completed	Title	Type of material	No. of pages (approx.)
Sept. 21	I Was a Teenage Werewolf	Novel	200
Sept. 25	The Collector of Moments	Picture Book	23
Sept. 30	The Ice Storm	Short Story	28

- A response should be as long as it needs to be for you to say what you want to say. Keep in mind, however, that useful reflection, problem-solving, and analysis require more than a few sentences to be effective.
- Your teacher will instruct you later on the kinds of entries you might make, supply you with sample cueing questions, outline the characteristics of effective responses, and even present a variety of sample responses.

For now, keep an up-to-date record of your reading.

Determine minimum requirements for reading responses

Before implementing response journals, teachers need to make some basic decisions about minimum requirements. Some key issues are outlined below.

How much should students be reading?

Ideally, students are part of an independent reading program, selecting material based on their interests, abilities, and stages of development. How much a student should be reading would vary from student to student. Personal response facilitates and supports this kind of diversity.

Most programs, however, are more prescribed and all students are often reading from the same text. In these cases, all students should have enough time to reach the minimum requirements. To avoid frustration in fluent readers and to keep them motivated and involved, you could have an independent reading component as part of any unit. The evaluation system could recognize students who do additional, self-selected, independent reading.

How often should students make written responses?

If there are too few responses, the processes of reflection and growth are hamstrung; if there are too many, the responses become perfunctory and superficial. Many teachers find that a response every second period or three responses a week strike a reasonable balance. Flexibility is essential. As circumstances and interest change, so should the minimum requirements.

How extensive should the responses be?

Students want to know the expectations. For many students, saying that a response should be as long as it needs to be is guidance enough. Teachers would prefer that the form fit the function. On the other hand, the oft-heard "How long does it have to be?" is a valid question. Since a student needs to respond in-depth and with some detail, little can be accomplished in two or three sentences. By the same token, length in and of itself is no indicator of quality. Responses that ramble on for pages retelling the plot in intricate detail are hardly worth the effort.

An easy and time-honored answer is that a response should be at least half a page and, of course, dependent on the size of the writing, whether or not the response is hand written or word-processed, and what the capabilities of the individual student are.

The other half of the equation is that the response can also be as long as it has to be. If they have something valid to say, students should be encouraged to say it, regardless of length.

What are the criteria for marking responses to reading?

Students need to know in language they can understand on what basis their responses will be judged and how they can improve their performance.

Journal entries should *always* meet the following criteria. They should (1) track daily reading, (2) track cumulative reading (reading inventories), (3) meet length requirements, for example, half a page, and (4) meet frequency requirements — three responses a week are recommended. On the other hand, retelling the plot, a pivotal feature of most classroom book reports, is a low-level thinking skill, at best, and should be included in responses only for specific and identifiable purposes.

Students should strive to make a variety of responses. Sometimes, journal entries should do the following:

- retell the plot
- relate real-life, related experiences
- explain how an individual's own experiences added to understanding
- predict what might happen next
- give reasons for predictions
- link *what* happens with *why* it happens
- separate fact from opinion
- comment on why characters act the way they do
- recognize patterns of behavior
- identify recurring images or descriptions
- talk about what the author's purposes might be
- support opinions with evidence from the story (e.g., incidents, images, character's actions or decisions)

Teachers also need to decide whether they're going to limit personal response to reading. Some teachers choose to start with responses to reading and possibly extend personal response into other areas later. Others may want to implement responses to reading, media, and small-group discussions immediately. Evaluation would need to incorporate all these elements.

Should private writing be part of personal response?

One other issue needs to be resolved before teachers launch a personal response program: the place of private writing.

Personal response is often confused with private writing; and that confusion is understandable. When journals first became popular in classrooms, they provided a forum for privileged, non-threatening dialogue, primarily with the teacher. In these journals, students could monitor and express their own "inner dialogues" as they reacted either to issues and events from the classroom curriculum and the wider world or to the significant experiences and emotions arising from their personal and private lives. This free-flowing "dialogue" could also be extended to teachers as students felt a need to include others in their thoughts and deliberations.

Sometimes students wrote to teachers for advice, while at other times they needed only a sympathetic and trusted reader. When teachers responded, they often wrote right in the students' journals. Other teachers thoughtfully used separate pieces of paper or Post-it notes to let students decide whether or not to retain the reply in the journal. In any event, the journal acted as a safety valve for students, allowing them to tap powerful feelings and, when they were in the grip of serious and often confusing personal problems, to express those feelings to someone else.

When using response journals, teachers need to decide whether or not to maintain the function of private writing. Caution is in order. At one time, teachers could use their own discretion when deciding what to do about student disclosures. In many jurisdictions, teachers are now legally required to report any suspicion of abuse, harassment, or worrisome behavior.

If teachers are going to include this private component into the public technique of personal response, a few basic guidelines need to be observed.

- Students must be reassured that in spite of existing routines for reading response journals, teachers will always welcome and read a private entry at any time, if the student feels it's pressing and important enough to hand in.
- Such entries should be clearly marked **Private**.
- Private entries should never be included in the evaluation of the writing folders.
- With writing of a private nature, teachers should respond in the role of trusted adult. In this role, teachers may often walk a tightrope with their comments. They need to advise, but not command; disagree, but not reject; sympathize, but not condone. They should see themselves as adult friends responding to student friends.
- Students *must* be advised that private entries *will* be passed on to school administrators if they reveal situations in which the student or others may come to harm.

For teachers who decide to implement these kinds of private journal entries along with the system of personal response as outlined throughout this book, the following student guideline serves as an introduction.

Student Guideline

Responding to Personal Issues

Everyone needs a friend to talk to. But you don't have to have a friend in order to sort out what's on your mind. You can talk about your thoughts and feelings with yourself and with your teacher in your response journal.

Remember to mark **_Private_** in your response journal whenever you want to write in this fashion. Your private entries will usually never be shown to anyone else without your permission and will not be considered when your journal is marked.

When you decide to write this way, find a quiet spot and don't concern yourself with mechanics or neatness or even how well or how poorly you're wording your thoughts. Even a poorly worded entry will get you in touch with your own thoughts and feelings and show you how you felt at a certain time — and that's the point of this kind of writing. Focus on the issue or feeling or idea and write whatever comes to mind. If you need a focus in order to begin, here are some suggestions.

- Explain your inner feelings. Try to put those feelings, good or bad, into words. This process can help you understand how your emotions work.

- Work out your problems. If you write about your worries, you may be able to understand more clearly what causes them.

- Explore ideas about life. Describe things you've noticed about people and the way they live. Discuss your ideas of right and wrong. Tell what you think is important in life.

- If you have something you want to write about, but don't know how to begin, try one of these phrases to get you going:

  Right now I feel . . .
  Sometimes, I wonder if . . .
  Some day, I'm going to . . .
  I hate it when . . .

If you want your teacher to read and reply to what you've written, simply hand it in and ask for a response. Unless you indicate otherwise, your teacher will reply on a separate, loose-leaf page or a Post-it note. That way you have the option of keeping or not keeping the reply in your response journal.

Be sure to remember, although teachers will usually respect your confidences, private entries _will_ be passed on to school administrators if they reveal situations in which you or others may come to harm.

Private issues can emerge at any time. For example, one student began a response to a novel and immediately related a traumatic personal experience triggered by the reading. Recently transferred into a regular English classroom from an ESL (English as a Second Language) program, the student was grappling with expression in English, with the concept of personal response, with the issue of privacy, and with the impact of personal experiences that had transformed his life.

Even though the class had been cautioned about how certain kinds of revelations would be handled, the student desperately needed this outlet for his emotions.

Response to Group Homes from Outer Space, *by Beth Goobie, Dec. 11*

Private!!!!!

I've nothing special to tell about the story. I only thought when I read this story, about when I was small, because the same thing happened to me that happened to Froggy. Her father would always hurt her, she would always cry, and her father would hit her for no reason, just because he was unhappy. Now it's just same with me, my father always hits me and I always cry, and if I cry more, my father hits me more. I can remember one time when I was eating supper, I wasn't very hungry, so I ate very slow, and my father hit me with his stick, just because I was eating slow. He didn't hit me just once, he hit many times until he was tired. He didn't just hit me, he hit my brother too. He hit him a lot harder than me. I remember the part that was so sad I could never forget it. My brother was breathing so hard and my father keep on hitting him until my mother yelled at him to stop and she hid his stick. That night I was crying so hard that I couldn't stop. Sometimes I hate my father very much. The reasons he hits me: business is bad, I eat soup slow, he's unhappy, he shouts at me, and I shout right back at him.

"Aaron" (age 11)

As this entry so dramatically illustrates, personal response reinforces the role of writing as an essential element in the processing of experience. Through personal response, the links between vicarious and real experiences, memory and reality, and cognitive and affective behaviors are uncovered, traced, and examined in idiosyncratic, recursive, unpredictable, and powerful ways.

At this point, you have done the groundwork for establishing a personal response program. You have chosen to implement those features of response journals that best suit your program, you have a clear sense of how your students have used journal writing in the past, and you have introduced some of the basic routines and established some of the fundamental requirements. Your students are now ready to apply the technique in a more defined and comprehensive manner.

The next chapter explains in detail how to focus this dynamic technique to enhance, expand, and deepen the study of reading and literature.

3

Responding in reading and literature programs

If students were to define reading by what they do in classrooms, many would say it's reading a story and answering questions.

This perception is borne out by elementary school practices. Beginning in the primary grades, students are introduced to the routine of answering main idea, supporting details, and vocabulary questions. Somewhere in the junior grades, they are also introduced to terms such as theme, plot, setting, climax, and character study. By that time, the entire class is ready to read the same novel, chapter by chapter, answering questions as they go along. The students' comprehension is largely measured by rating their answers to teacher-made tests that stress plot recall, application of literary terms, vocabulary, and written fluency.

When they reach secondary school, students are usually treated as blank slates, reintroduced to the same, tried and true English catechism, and cranked through an arbitrarily chosen selection of texts, one by one. To make matters worse, many are expected to worship a Shakespearean play they usually glimpse, however faintly, with the help of a "translation" and set of study notes purchased at the local paperback bookstore.

Why is teaching reading by asking questions a problem?

We've known for almost two decades that the question-and-answer approach to developing reading skills is arbitrary, repetitive, and unproductive. As Richard Allington puts it: "Asking questions does little to foster thinking and question answering provides little good evidence of understanding." Yet this "method" remains the preferred and most common way of teaching reading in schools today.

To understand the dynamic of traditional questioning in a reading program, try this simple test. Read the following poem excerpt and answer the questions.

25

Jabberwocky

'Twas brillig, and the slithy toves
Did gyre and gimble in the wabe.
All mimsy were the borogroves,
And the mome raths outgrabe.

(From *Through the Looking Glass* by Lewis Carroll)

1. What was the time?
2. Where were the toves?
3. What were the toves doing?
4. How were the borogroves feeling?
5. Choose the best meaning for "slithy."
   a. hungry
   b. slimy and lithe
   c. disappointed and angry
   d. afraid

You can easily answer the four so-called comprehension questions and the "vocabulary" question lies transparent to an educated guess. Anyone should score at least 80 percent on this reading test. On the other hand, for a genuine test of comprehension, take pencil and paper and illustrate what you understand from the poem.

As the example above demonstrates, understanding isn't necessary. The answers to many traditional reading comprehension questions can be derived from syntax alone.

Why then has this type of questioning endured for so long?

Part of the answer lies in a belief in simplicity. Language arts/English teaching remains in the vice-like grip of reductionism. In this view, a complex system, such as reading, can be broken into its constituent parts and explained by these simplified fragments and the interactions between them.

According to reductionism, the logical way to teach reading is to start with the simple constituents and gradually build them into a complex whole. Advocates of a phonics approach to the teaching of reading would start with single graphemes, build them into words, connect words into phrases and sentences, and link sentences into paragraphs.

While neat and logical and subject to simple teaching and accountability, reductionism is subject to one major problem. When applied to a complex system, such as reading, it doesn't work. In the natural world, reductionism explains simple systems, such as eclipses or the motions of planets; however, it fails dismally with complex systems, such as understanding and predicting the human genome.

The theory does offer something constructive. Early readers benefit from some grounding in simple fundamentals, such as learning the alphabet and applying initial consonant recognition to new vocabulary. That's not enough, however. Language systems are too complex to be unravelled in such simplistic terms, and learners are too individual to be able to use the same entry points into fluency. Students don't grow into readers on a reductionist's assembly line running in reverse.

Many teachers and parents still favor the question-and-answer approach because of its easy accountability. By treating reading as a series of right and wrong answers applied to an arbitrarily chosen series of requisite texts, teachers are able to process and package reading results much like bread dough in a factory. The learning is prescribed in scope and sequence, standardized, teacher-directed and evaluated, and easily described and managed.

No wonder so many children develop a resistance to and difficulties with the reading process. For reading to flourish in a classroom as a dynamic, creative, open-ended, problem-solving activity, the cycle of read these pages/answer these questions needs to be permanently broken.

What are effective reading practices?

In his remarkable book on reading, *Better Than Life*, Daniel Pennac claims: "You can't make people read. Any more than you can make them love, or dream." He's right. You may not be able to make people read, but you *can* assist them on their journey to becoming better readers.

Specific reading practices have been demonstrated over time to be highly effective. Depending on the grade level you teach, the number of administratively prescribed components in your programs, or matters of budget or class size, you may choose to exclude or be unable to include some of these elements. If too many of these components are missing, however, significant student and teacher frustration with the program is inevitable.

The following questions highlight effective reading practices. As you reflect on your own reading program, consider how many of these questions you can answer in the affirmative.

- Does the program feature frequent and regular readalouds of both fiction and non-fiction by the teacher?
- Are there enough materials to match individual student interests and abilities?
- Do the students have frequent opportunities to select their own materials (and not just from a range picked by the teacher)?
- Are students provided with regular and significant amounts of in-class time to read (as opposed to answering questions based on their reading)?
- Do students have frequent opportunities to respond to materials in a personally significant manner (not just in ways dictated by the teacher or in response to questions asked by the teacher)?
- Do students have many opportunities to discuss with someone else what they're reading? Do they seek out and value peer opinions and advice?
- Does the program include the flexibility to allow students to employ a variety of strategies to comprehend material (e.g., retelling, predicting, relating to personal experience, reflecting, discussing, dramatizing, expanding on the text, comparing, hypothesizing, making inferences and judgments)?
- Is the reading program an integral part of an integrated language arts/English program?

The direction for effective reading classrooms springs from research into the attitudes and skills that separates a "good" reader from a "struggling" one. The "good" reader profile establishes specific guidelines for programming. Highly effective reading programs, for example, are built on diversity and choice. Students are offered a variety of reading and discussion opportunities and are encouraged to respond to their reading in multiple and personally significant ways. Students in effective programs also learn that reflection is the key to comprehension and risk taking the hallmark of an accomplished, independent reader. An ineffective program, on the other hand, limits choice and reflection and forces students to become dependent on teachers to lead them through an artificial, illogical, test-strewn maze.

Why take class time for reading?

Reading is a purposeful and natural activity. We read for enjoyment, to pursue personal interests, to investigate all aspects of our lives, and to solve all manner of problems. We read to understand and to help cope with our world. As the writing process in the classroom tries to reflect the dynamics of writing in the real world, so the reading process must reflect the dynamics of reading in the real world. Just as we learn to write by writing, not by learning about writing, so we learn to read by reading, not by learning about reading.

In the case of many students, outside of class, they read as little as possible or not at all. Since proficiency can be developed only through the act of reading itself, in-class time to read is fundamental to any reading program at any level.

Reading in class also validates the experience. If the teacher allots precious class time to independent reading, students are keenly aware that it's a valued activity. In-class reading also allows the teacher to monitor the myriad reading behaviors present in any class group, offering advice, encouragement, enrichment, or remediation as needed. The practice of in-class reading should be carefully structured to include these components:

- a regular, significant amount of time to read, such as 20 to 30 minutes each day or at least 90 minutes per week
- the teacher modelling enjoyment and focused reading of self-selected materials at the same time as students at least once or twice per week
- a method of tracking and rewarding in-class reading, as well as reading accomplished privately
- a relaxed and inviting setting conducive to reading including relatively quiet, undisturbed stretches of time, the option to sit on the floor or in hallways, or the presence of a rug or comfortable chairs

Response journals offer a fast, efficient way to track independent reading. As students realize that independent reading is rewarded in the evaluation system, they become willing partners in developing a routine of regular reading at school and at home. That kind of habitual, focused reading not only helps make them better readers but also supplies a rich and varied context for reflecting and responding in their journals. As the reflective investigation into their reading experiences deepens and produces added insight, students are further motivated to maintain their independent reading practices. The tracking function of journals encourages students to read more; the more they read, the more ideas and questions they bring to their journal entries.

Reading should always highlight meaning

Through their classroom experiences, students construct an intrinsic sense of what it means to read in school. Any number of conceptions can develop over time, depending on how the various aspects of reading have been emphasized. Even in the intermediate division, for instance, some students equate successful reading with oral fluency; for many others, successful reading is measured by marks attained on a report card.

Since student perceptions of reading are determined by the myriad day-to-day reading tasks they encounter, teachers should consciously and continuously monitor their programs to ensure that meaning is consistently emphasized.

In their hectic multi-tasking world, for example, teachers need to realize that while routines establish order, they often substitute form for function. As a case in point, the following outline represents a common pattern in reading instruction. On Monday, the teacher introduces a short story and the class silently reads it. On Tuesday, students complete vocabulary exercises derived from the story. The vocabulary is taken up on Wednesday and comprehension questions assigned. The following day, the comprehension questions are taken up and enrichment questions or activities assigned. On Friday, the students complete a test on the story and the enrichment activities are either taken up or collected for marking. While students are focused and productive in this kind of cycle, the format itself may be hindering their efforts to engage meaningfully with the text.

Teachers can gauge how effectively their programs emphasize meaning in the light of these questions:

- How are students helped to comprehend text while they are actively reading?
- How and how often are students enabled to discuss their reading with someone else?
- How can they ask their own questions about their reading without risk of embarrassment or of being judged inadequate?
- How do seatwork activities support an individual's attempts to comprehend material?
- What seatwork activities would function more effectively before or during rather than after the actual reading?
- How many of the assigned tasks are meant to monitor whether or not the students have accomplished the reading as opposed to facilitating the comprehension process?

The words on a page only become meaningful when infused with experience, real or vicarious. A manual on sailing a boat, for example, explodes with meaning once you've actually sailed. In the same way, a picture can illuminate a thousand words written about Niagara Falls. Comprehension is directly affected by an individual's experiences and the beliefs and values developed from those experiences.

To become successful readers, students need to learn open-ended strategies that help build bridges between their own experiences and the texts that confront them. The role of reader can be dynamic, liberating, and self-determining, if enough strategies, such as the following, are adopted:

- relating to personal experience, such as life experiences or other vicarious experiences from books and media, and integrating personal understanding with the text's constructed experience
- using personal response to make comparisons and inferences and to expand on the text
- hypothesizing, such as predicting plot and character development
- distinguishing cause-and-effect relationships
- distinguishing fact from opinion
- recognizing central meanings, patterns, and motifs
- identifying the attributes and tendencies of characters and how they impact on the story
- using incidents, image motifs, and significant details to establish and build a meaning structure and support judgments

While personal response theory is the engine that drives the use of response journals, all of these strategies have a role to play in a fully functioning, personal response program. In the course of using their journals to reflect on and analyze their reading, students select the most appropriate strategies, singly or in combination, to unlock the meaning encapsulated in a particular text.

Given the diversity of many of our school populations, students constantly need to discover personal ways of bridging the gaps between their own cultures and backgrounds and the often unfamiliar cultures and settings they meet in books and movies. One student found a unique entry point from her own experiences into the unfamiliar world and time of *Tom's Midnight Garden*, the filmed serialization of the novel by Philippa Pearce. The plot turns on the magical transformation of a garden beside an old Victorian mansion in rural England.

The student response below reveals how naturally and idiosyncratically personal response evolves.

Response to Tom's Midnight Garden, *by Philippa Pearce (Filmed serialization, first segment),* April 16

This movie is about Tom who has to go to his uncle's house because his brother, Peter, has the measles. They are in England, so they drive on the left side and the steering wheel is on the right side just like when I was in Trinidad. At Tom's uncle's house, it has bars on the windows and Tom doesn't like that. You would feel like you were in a cage. They also had that in Trinidad. My sister didn't like that either. She asked our uncle, "Are the bars there to keep the scary people out?"

Our uncle said, "Maybe it's to keep the scary people in."

The movie also looks old-fashioned like the 50's.

I still want to keep watching to see what's wrong with that clock and which door Tom goes through to get to the garden.

Kelly (age 13)

Literature promotes the making and sharing of meaning

All teachers, by necessity and regardless of subject area and grade level, are reading teachers. Sometime during the middle school years (grades 6–10), however, some teachers assume they are no longer reading teachers, but

30

teachers of literature. Along with this responsibility comes the task of transmitting to students the correct interpretation of whatever piece of literature the teacher chooses and which every student in the class must study.

Many teachers of middle school students make two crucial assumptions: (1) they assume that they no longer need to attend to their students' reading development and (2) they assume that the teaching of literature is somehow different from the teaching of reading. These assumptions have commonly spawned unreasonable teacher expectations, frustrating practices, and the growth of an elitist mentality in the one area of the curriculum that should be universally liberating and enlightening.

Let's examine the issue of how long students need support in learning to read.

Even as children enter Kindergarten, a gap is already apparent between those who have an obvious facility with reading and those who are diagnosed "at risk" of developing reading difficulties and, consequently, of "falling behind." As children move through their school years, that gap only grows larger, with students at all levels ranging along a spectrum of varying attitudes toward and facility with reading.

The work of learning in schools is not just language-based, but literacy-based. The more proficient you are at reading or writing, the more able you are to handle school tasks. Regardless of grade level, teachers can never assume that all students possess the requisite reading skills. All teachers, especially at the intermediate and secondary school levels, have to acknowledge and attend to that range. While reading and learning are not synonymous, as students move through the grades success in school and reading fluency become intrinsically linked: there is an increasing reliance on a text-driven curriculum.

The raison d'être of teachers and schools is to facilitate learning. To assume that all students read alike inherently subverts the learning process. The business of teachers and schools, therefore, centres on the teaching of reading. Locked into a rigid, traditional model of instruction, however, too many English teachers are frustrated by their inability to manipulate an implacable syllabus to fit the needs of their students.

Reading is the interactive and reciprocal process of making and sharing meaning; not at all coincidentally, that's what literature is all about. In both cases, readers try to make sense of an author's vision and consider any implications in that vision for themselves.

Although students can benefit from help, they need to begin the search for meaning themselves. Students need to be persuaded that learning begins not with the answer arrived at by the teacher or in the reference text written by a famous critic, but rather in their own feelings, experiences, and thoughts. They need to chart, explore, and analyze their own reactions, not study tips to help them regurgitate someone else's words. It's important that they see the study of literature as an opportunity to learn more about themselves and the world around them, and not as a series of hurdles to overcome.

Young people can learn a lot from literature. A piece of literature has the power to touch young readers emotionally and intellectually, stimulating reflection, and encouraging inner change. An author's vision can help them illuminate, reassess, and possibly redirect what they believe, what they value, and how they conduct their lives.

As they read, students learn many things that they can apply to their own lives. They see how others cope with disappointment, confusion, and frustration; as well, they discover that they aren't alone in feeling inadequate about their bodies, their abilities, or their social graces. They learn about discrimination, such as racism, sexism, or homophobia and how these emerge. Through fiction, young people also augment their sense of the range of acceptable interpersonal behaviors, including dealing with sexual urges and the intricacies of dating customs.

Literature, in essence, explains us to ourselves, allowing us to mine and refine the past, interpret the present, and predict the future. Through literature, we examine our parameters, study our strengths and weaknesses, and test our potential.

Personal response unlocks literature

The connections between life and literature have long fascinated both writers and readers. Writers attempt to craft from their own experiences intellectually constructed, vicarious realities that will involve and move their readers. When readers are involved in and moved by a literary creation, they are intrigued by the associations they invariably make between that creation and their own lives. The matrix created by the reciprocal relationship between real life and fiction is the focus for the study of literature in schools.

Students are required to assess the impact of a fictional work and determine how it was created by sorting out and describing the components of that fictional world and then delineating the elements that have relevance for their own reality. In this regard, the challenge becomes one of explicating a piece of fiction from the differing perspectives of both reader and writer. How do students separate their emotional responses to material as readers from the task of intellectual deconstruction of a writer's manipulations? Where do they start? How do they proceed?

T. S. Eliot proposed that literature could be understood both emotionally and intellectually. If the writing were constructed skillfully enough, he believed it would produce a universal emotional understanding in readers even without an intellectual appreciation of how that effect was created. Combined with an intellectual appreciation, of course, the impact of the writing could be exquisitely intensified. As a first step in explicating a literary work, personal response encourages students to acknowledge, describe, and interpret that kind of emotional understanding.

Emotional understanding comes naturally to us. Imagine the sense of inner tranquillity evoked by an early morning walk in spring beside a quiet lake, blue sky above and the sun dancing on the water. If you set out to analyze and explain that feeling, where would you start? If someone didn't feel the same way you did about that morning, how much of your experience could you convey and how much could they appreciate? In times of deepest contemplation, we might attempt to trace the myriad internal and external factors that united to produce such a sublime emotional response. More often than not, however, we share a heartfelt "Hey, what a great morning!" and allow our feelings to unconsciously sort out the experience.

Much more is required of students immersed in the study of literature. Through their response journals, students set out to unravel the mysteries of a literary work, first by detecting and mapping out their own observable emotional reactions to it and then using those findings to trace the intellectual plan of the work that produced them. That plan, unfortunately, is never as linear, straightforward, nor as transparent as we might assume.

Authors write to "pick away at" and make sense of their world and themselves. Their writing is often a journey of discovery through a darkened, amorphous mansion with a thousand different doors opening into thousands of different, interconnected rooms. They choose one "door" to get inside: perhaps a character flaw or a resonant image or a compelling, time-worn theme. They turn on the lights in the first room, assess what's about them, and see where the next door will lead them. Countless surprises, illuminations, and insights await them. Sometimes the world they discover is more than they realize or completely understand.

As readers, we come to a book with our own distinctly individual and uniquely personal perspectives, including variables of language, background, and interests. No one book can attract or serve everyone at the same time and in the same way. When we do begin with a common experience, whatever we value or are intrigued by or are confused by in that experience will vary depending on the individual. In other words, we all need to find our personal portals. Otherwise, the "doorway" that leads one student into a book's heart could turn out to be a cul de sac for another. The study of literature is not a search for a single, unalterable vision of an author's intentions.

Take the example of what happens when you see and discuss a film with a friend. When you begin to comment on your feelings about the film, where you start seems totally reasonable and relevant to you. However, it may appear obscure to your friend.

The discussion proceeds in fits and starts, jumping here, there, and everywhere, as you both follow, share, and extend your own personal paths of perception, importance, and logic. A color motif might strike you while a recurring shape or image might catch your friend's attention. Your friend might focus on a similar, real-life experience while you've become distracted by a personal phobia encountered in the film. Eventually, you arrive at a heightened appreciation of the film and an understanding of the other person's point of view, even though you might still disagree about the film.

The study of literature in schools needs to follow a similar exploratory route. When students become convinced that it provides an opportunity to learn more about themselves and the world around them, they will actively search for meaning, starting with their own feelings and experiences. With help, they will learn how to chart and explore those beginnings. Later, they will be able to step back and analyze the entire process.

The different ways that Baz Lurhmann's film version of *Romeo and Juliet* can be used serve as a useful illustration. Teachers often use the film as an enticing entry point for the play; others use the film as a super-charged review after studying the play. The film's potential for exciting and informing the learning process, however, can be easily blunted, especially if an essay comparing and contrasting the two versions becomes that evening's homework.

Students first need an opportunity to identify and explore their own, personal entry points and to discover where they may lead. One student might start by extolling the virtues of Leonardo de Caprio and eventually centre in on essential elements of the tragic romance. Another might question the way Mercutio was portrayed as sexually ambivalent and end with an appreciation of the character's hot-blooded passion and destructive violence. Depending on the individual, the gangs, the parties, the parents, the sea-side setting, and numerous other entry points lead to a genuine, reflective recognition of the links that join film/play to viewer/reader.

Comprehension rests in the mind, not on the page or screen. The depth of our understanding as we read is dependent on the experiences, attitudes, values, and skills we bring to the reading. The study of literature rests on the assumption that life and literature inform one another. By comparing our own experiences with the vicarious experiences found in a book, we can expand and deepen the understandings we have of our own lives.

At the heart of our understandings lies the concept of personal response. In an interactive and reciprocal manner, our real-life understandings can unlock and expose the purpose and significance of a piece of literature. In any reading experience, a student begins the search for meaning by monitoring the feelings and memories that are stirred and stimulated in response to the reading. As the student sorts through these responses and explores the reasons behind them, new entry points are subtly forged back into the material. The shifting dynamic back and forth gradually illuminates both the text and the reader's own life.

Literature is independent, reflective reading and its study a life skill. The study of literature has often been considered an end in itself; we need to convince our students that it's a powerful and liberating "means."

Cueing questions promote personal responses to reading

If you ask independent readers to respond to a text in a personally significant manner, they can do it. They possess the confidence, skills, and understanding of the reading process necessary to follow their own idiosyncratic routes through material.

Most students, however, remain dependent on the teacher for direction and guidance. They merely want the teacher to tell them what to do. They need help in developing an ability to make personal responses.

Once students know the routines of keeping a response journal and have begun tracking their reading in journals, you can guide them in understanding the nature of personal response. They'll be ready for "cueing" questions that will prompt them into their first responses.

The next student guideline, "Personal Response — More Than a Book Report," addresses the content of responses.

Most students tend to see the function of a reading, viewing, or listening experience as matching a prescribed set of answers someone else knows to a prescribed set of questions someone else devises. A prescribed set of questions, unfortunately, often produces perfunctory or formulaic responses. The teacher's goal is to assist these students to develop an independent reader's approach to exploring material.

Such students may appreciate a few model or sample questions to cue their initial efforts. Gradually, as they better understand how individual a personal response needs to be, these students will accept more and more responsibility for the direction of their responses.

Student Guideline

Personal Response — More Than a Book Report

Responding in your journal is different than writing a book report.

In a typical book report, you comment on the whole book. You might explain where the story takes place, describe some of the main characters, and briefly relate the main events. You might conclude by revealing what most appealed to you about the story and how well it captured and maintained your interest. You might even use a rating scale from 0–10 or give the book a number of "thumbs up."

When it comes to responding in your journal, most of the time, you'll be thinking and writing about your reading before you've finished the book. Sometimes, you may have read only 10 or 15 pages. You will also be expected to consider and explain not just how you feel about characters and events but *why* you feel that way. A significant part of your evaluation will be based on how fully, thoughtfully, and insightfully you examine your own feelings as you read.

Your teacher will give you a list of questions designed to help you get started. Please remember that the questions are meant only to guide you into thinking and writing about your reading in the following ways:

- explaining why you were reminded of experiences in your own life or in other stories in books, the movies, or TV as you read;
- explaining how your own experiences were the same as or different from those in the book and how they added to your understanding of the book's characters or events;
- predicting before you read ahead what characters might do, how events might unfold, and explain why you made those predictions;
- linking up *what* happens with *why* it happens that way (cause and effect)
- separating what is factual in the story from the characters' and author's personal opinions;
- identifying the aspects of characters' personalities and behavior that lead them to make certain kinds of decisions or take certain actions;
- recognizing the author's purpose in telling this story, the recurring images or repetitions in descriptions, or the patterns that become apparent in the way characters think and behave;
- using incidents, patterns in images or description, and significant decisions or actions to support your opinions about the story, the characters, and the ideas the author wants you to reflect on.

Cueing questions, such as those that appear in the next two guidelines, form an intermediate step. By self-selecting the question or questions most applicable to their own material and personal leanings, students gain a greater appreciation of what a personally significant response is all about. The cueing questions act as models on which students will eventually base the formulation of their own questions.

Eventually, as students are weaned from an unbudging reliance on a list of questions, they will become more independent as readers and begin to accept their own autonomy in the reading process. At that point, they are ready to assume responsibility for the direction of their inquiries into literature.

For the first response opportunities, focusing on a few selected, open-ended questions is preferable to a longer list that students may find intimidating or confusing. "Making a Personal Response" is designed to get students started. After the first few responses, teachers can introduce the second student guideline, "More Cueing Questions," to demonstrate and support a wider range of options.

When students begin responding to material in a personally significant manner, their initial efforts will reflect their diverse backgrounds, experiences, attitudes, and abilities. The range in the quantity, complexity, and sophistication of the writing is often startling. Naturally, as students become more familiar and confident with the technique, their responses will become more spontaneous and personally evocative.

These next three responses, for instance, came from the same classroom. Freed from answering specific questions about the stories or writing to a prescribed length, the responses ranged from brief, personal anecdotes to extended, multifaceted discourses. The students were unfamiliar with the technique of personal response and had not been given cueing questions. After a brief explanation, they were asked to respond to a readaloud.

The teacher read aloud two stories from Louis Sachar's extraordinary collection, *Sideways Stories from Wayside School*. The first story revolves around a boy who could only read books upside down and the second involves a boy named Nancy.

If you've never encountered Sideways Stories from Wayside School, by the way, run immediately to a bookstore; students from primary through to the early intermediate grades love the stories!

Responses to Sideways Stories from Wayside School, *by Louis Sachar pages 6–18, Feb. 21*

When I heard this story, it reminded me of my second grade class when we switched names.

Raymond (age 12)

The story was really funny. I've never heard of someone reading their book upside down or the other story with a guy named Nancy. But I have a guy's name, too, even though I'm a girl. My name's Bobbi and it's kind of like a guy's name and people always spell my name wrong. They spell it Bobby when it's Bobbi.

This book also reminds me of my cousin. She can't tell the difference between left and right, so she puts her shoes on the wrong feet. In grade 8 we read very serious books and we don't read humorous books like this book. It was a good change. I really enjoyed this book and look forward to reading more of Louis Sachar's books.

Bobbi (age 12)

36

Student Guideline

Making a Personal Response

As you read, you think about what's happening in your book in many different ways. Sometimes, questions come to your mind about some of the characters and how they are behaving. At other times, you might be impressed by the way someone or something was described. You might even be reminded of something similar that happened to you or to someone you know.

After reading independently today, try to describe the kinds of impressions that your reading has inspired and note any questions it has raised. You may find the following questions useful in guiding your responses. Bear in mind that they are only suggestions. You don't have to answer these questions if you have a better way to write about your reading experience.

- After reading this far, what more do you hope to learn about what these characters plan to do, what they think, feel, and believe, or what happens to them?

- As you think ahead to your next day's reading, what possible directions might the story take? How do you hope the story will unfold?

- If the setting and characters were changed to reflect your own neighborhood and friends and acquaintances, how would the events of the story have to change and why would that be so?

- Do you wish that your own life was more like the lives of the people in the story you're reading or that the people you know were more like those in the story? In what ways would you like the real world to be more like the world of your book? In what ways are you glad they're different?

More Cueing Questions

Now that you've begun responding, you may have found that the original list of cueing questions didn't quite fit the book you were reading or what you wanted to say about it. The following questions give you more choices.

Keep in mind, however, that when you're ready, you can dispense with these questions and write about your reading as you see fit. If you do, use the guideline "Personal Response: More Than a Book Report" to ensure that your responses are on the right track.

Remember that the following questions are suggestions only and are intended for students who *choose* to use them.

- As you think ahead to your next day's reading, what possible directions might the story take? How do you hope the story will unfold?
- What surprised you about the section you read today? How does this change affect what might happen next in the story?
- As you read today, what feelings did you experience in response to events or characters (e.g., irritation, wonder, disbelief, recognition, dislike), and why do you think you responded this way?
- What questions do you hope to have answered next day as you read more of this story?
- What startling/unusual/effective words, phrases, expressions, or images did you come across in your reading today that you would like to have explained or clarified? Which ones would you like to use in your own writing?
- Have you ever had a dream or daydream that seemed similar to an event or theme in this book? Try to describe the dream or daydream and trace the parallels.
- After reading this far, what more do you hope to learn about what these characters plan to do, what they think, feel, believe, or what happens to them?
- With what characters do you identify most closely or feel the most sympathy for? What is it about these characters that makes you feel this way?
- How much do you personally agree or disagree with the way various characters think and act and the kinds of beliefs and values they hold? Where do you differ and why?
- What issues in this story are similar to real-life issues that you've thought about or had some kind of experience with? How has the story clarified or confused or changed your views on any of these issues?
- What characters and situations in the story remind you of people and situations in your own life? How are they similar and how do they differ?
- How did the characters or events in this book remind you of characters or events in other books you've read or movies or television shows you've seen? Do you prefer one of these treatments over the others? If so, why?

I really enjoyed this book because it is completely eccentric and out of the ordinary. These qualities to me are enviable because once in a while I would like my normal and conservative school to be fun and exciting, not to mention odd, like Wayside School. This wacky atmosphere would benefit the school because things and events would liven up.

It seems as if new and weird things are happening all the time! One of the main reasons why I like these stories is because of the way they are written. For example, when John was upside down and standing on his head, the writing in the book was upside down, forcing the teacher to turn the book upside down to continue reading from it. This feature made the reading more amusing and interesting. I also envy this school because their teachers seem more lenient and easy-going. I wish our teachers were more like this sometimes.

Overall, I enjoyed this book because it is original and refreshingly different from the usual bland books our society reads. I think Louis Sachar is a brilliant author who writes enjoyable books for all ages!

Karen (age 12)

Personal response affords junior-grade students the opportunity to explore reading in the same spontaneous and open-ended way they naturally explore their world. In a relatively brief response, the following student adroitly connects her reading with a real-life experience, traces that personal anecdote back to another vicarious experience, and projects forward beyond the end of the book.

Response to Kit, the Adventures of a Raccoon, *by Shirley E. Woods Finished Jan. 23*

This book was telling the story of a raccoon's life from when Kit was a baby to when he was all grown up. When I read this book I felt sad because Kit's two sisters died. One died because an owl flew off with her. And the other one died because she got run over by a car. When I was six or seven, I had a fish named Wishy but then he died one morning. This reminds me of a book I read called Eric Is Allergic. *It is about a boy named Eric who is allergic to feathers, dog's and cat's, and other fur animals too. I wonder what happened to Kit's sister Tara after the owl flew off with her? I wonder what happened to Kit's other sister's body after Jess got run over by a car?*

Brittany (age 9)

Young people have no choice but to try to make sense of new experiences in the light of what they already know. In the next response, the young reader valiantly attempts to understand the issue of discrimination by relating an episode when she herself felt excluded. She also clearly articulates her unease at efforts to submerge a character's self-identity and culture. As with any inquiring reader, the more questions she answers, the more questions arise for her.

Response to Remember Me, *by Irene N. Watts pages 1–168, Feb. 2*

What I don't like about this book is Hitler and some other people. Reading the story made me feel sad because the Jewish were treated so badly. Once when we got to a theme park and I was really young, there wasn't anything I could do

39

because I was either too young or too short. This story is similar to another one which I read about Hitler and how badly he treated the Jewish. I wonder why Hitler hated the Jewish?

I also didn't like that her foster parents weren't what she was looking for. Her foster parents were too nice. And then her foster mother kept talking about Elizabeth her daughter who died when she was ten. Marianne had to stay in Elizabeth's room and in her bed and her foster mother put Elizabeth's hair tie in Marianne's hair and gave her ball to Marianne to play with and changed her name to Mairi and Marianne had to sleep with Elizabeth's doll.

Why did Marianne have to use all of Elizabeth's things? Why did her foster parents think of her as their actual daughter? I wonder why Marianne had to go to Sunday school when she was Jewish? Why did their next door neighbour not like the Jewish and why did she tell everyone on the street about Marianne being Jewish? Why did everyone on her street stare and whisper about her?

Alys (age 9)

Book publishers understand and exploit the link between experience and reading. They've learned that young people are apt to read more and, therefore, buy more books if they see themselves reflected in the material. Intrinsic interest initially motivates young people to read this kind of book; familiarity with the context allows them to unlock the meaning more easily. For this reason, book publishers commission writers to create characters and plots that resonate with the experiences and interests of a specific age group.

This formulaic approach, however, represents a double-edged sword. Growth in reading is developmental and dependent on emotional and intellectual factors. As students mature and develop a new perspective on this kind of age-focused material, they are able to distinguish its contrived and artificial characteristics.

The following intermediate response demonstrates how this kind of material has interest and impact, but only for a limited time.

Response to Why Just Me?, *by Martyn Godfrey*
pages 130–45, Jan. 2

I really like this book. It was funny, very interesting, and not too long. When I first started to read the book, I was amazed at how much I could relate to it.

At the beginning of last year, I felt somewhat scared of going to grade 7 because it would mean I'd have to mature and back then I liked my age and my maturity. The character in the book feels exactly the same way I did. She's scared and confused.

Now I'm not because it seems I've changed so much in one year. I'm completely different. That's why in some ways the book was a little boring because the girl was one year younger than me. I also thought the book was a little fake. At the end everything worked out perfectly and that never happens!

Samia H. (age 12)

In the next response, the same student discovers the added complexity and ambiguity in the more realistic characters, issues, and points of view she's looking for in a new series of novels. As she explores her reactions to the stories, she ventures far beyond recognizing the similarities and differences in her world and the world of the novel to a more insightful analysis of the characters' motivations.

Response to Clearwater Crossing: Heart and Soul, *by Laura Peyton Roberts pages 162–217, Jan. 9*

This was book three in the series and it definitely lived up to its standards. This book talks about a lot of different topics like religion, drinking, and popularity, but the thing I really liked was that instead of being one-sided about the situation, it gives you the point of view of all eight characters.

One thing I don't really like is the fact that the two books only discuss one religion, Christianity. They don't explore other religions and I really wish they had.

I think Jesse, Melanie, and Nicole's characters are the ones with the most problems. To me, it seems as if Jess had a drinking problem, but he doesn't want to admit it to himself. He hates his family life and his school life and he turns to alcohol. Nicole's character is really weird. She thinks there's only one way she can be and she seems to look into situations in a strange way. She wants to be exactly like Melanie. We still haven't read a lot about Melanie's past, but it seems she's changed a lot. I wish the author would talk more about Ben's character and his point of view. I know nothing about him.

Samia H. (age 12)

This final response illustrates how an objective, comprehensive analysis of reading material is subtly supported by an individual's emotional responses. The student follows her feelings through to a meaningful, intellectual understanding of the issues and themes embedded in the material. The conclusions she arrives at help her clarify and articulate her own attitudes and values.

Response to The Hiding-Place, *by Lyn Cook Finished April 7*

This book was beautifully written. All the questions were tied together and answered. Everything that happened in this story was important and came together to answer something at the end.

I've also learned a lot about things that happened at that time, like about the coureurs de bois and what they did, how life was in New France, what kinds of food they had, all the different Indian tribes and languages, how they hunted, and how people lived.

I was glad Michel came back, but it was sad when Star Boy wanted to leave and go back to his family. But, I guess if I was Star Boy I would want to go back to my home too. I think Star Boy understands that Justine wanted to help him and that she's his friend. I'm glad Justine made good friends with an enemy. If she knew he was an Iroquois right at the first, she might not have taken care of him. I'm glad that she found out about that later. That proves that if you don't know the enemy, they could become your friends.

I think Lyn Cook is a very talented writer. This story was very well planned. Michel was mentioned so much in the beginning, but then we forgot about him

41

and no one knew that he was going to be there at the end. Lyn makes the story so that everything is important and gives you clues to the answers to your questions.

I wonder if they'll ever see Star Boy again? I hope they do. I wonder if Star Boy would remember them? And I hope Justine makes friends with all the Iroquois.

Catherine (age 11)

Read aloud and let students respond

Students of all ages, from Kindergarten through secondary school, should be read to regularly, if not daily. When setting priorities, teachers need to establish readaloud times as essential components of their program.

People who are read to are more apt to read and more apt to enjoy reading enough to become lifelong readers. As students listen, they glean and savor stimulating examples of how language can be colored and flavored through individual interpretation. Through readalouds, the creative, subjective nature of reading is externalized. Readalouds also provide common experiences upon which discussion and analysis can focus.

We also learn about the special language of books by listening to books read aloud. Listening vocabularies are far greater than reading vocabularies. At any age, by listening to the compelling and intricate language of literature, often more difficult than we ourselves read, we develop an understanding of the rich and complex context within which our own reading expands and flourishes.

By the same token, expository material that attempts to persuade or inform has its own unique flavor and style directly related to the purpose for the writing. Since many teachers neglect exposition in their readaloud selections, we shouldn't be surprised when students have more difficulty reading and writing exposition than fiction. Part of the difficulty, of course, is that many content-related texts are poorly written. On the other hand, exposure has an impact. If we expect students to devote much of their in-school time reading and writing exposition, we need to inject a significant amount of expository material into our readaloud programs.

Items that strike a teacher's own interests or that intrigue or compel are always best. If a teacher reads a hoary "chestnut" from any genre out of a sense of duty, the lack of involvement will show. With non-fiction, teachers can feature newspaper and magazine articles and columns, expository material related to issues under discussion or study, and collections of contemporary and time-proven essays on a variety of themes.

In the same way, to support the reading, writing, and appreciation of poetry, teachers should regularly read poetry aloud. Reading aloud student-written material also supplies a powerful stimulus to and validation of the classroom writing program.

Some teachers have had great success with picture books for older students. Among the many extraordinary books for junior or intermediate readers are these: *Brother Eagle, Sister Sky,* with paintings by Susan Jeffers, for instance, introduces students to a Native American's perspective on the sanctity of nature through the words of Chief Seattle; *Piggybook*, by Anthony Browne, explores the issue of sexism in a novel and ironic manner; and *To Hell with Dying*, by Alice Walker, celebrates the ability of love to maintain and transform human relationships.

Whatever the genre, teachers should choose readaloud material that they personally believe is noteworthy. They should also like the material themselves and enjoy reading it aloud. The material might be a personal favorite, a well-written account of a controversial issue, or a "classic" piece of literature. Whatever it is, a specific purpose in reading the material aloud is the first step. The next step is for teachers to be so familiar with the material that they feel comfortable "performing" it.

With fiction, teachers often include poetry, short stories, and either excerpts from novels or a "sure-fire" novel in instalments. Selection when using a single novel is crucial; a good rule is to choose a novel the reader can't wait to open each day. After a few sessions, on the other hand, if students don't feel the same way, it's time to choose another. Never struggle through a readaloud that hasn't found an appreciative audience; there's nothing to gain and everything to lose.

A well-rounded readaloud inventory would include the following:

- picture books
- poetry
- fiction, including novels and short stories
- exposition, including essays, newspaper and magazine articles, and information-based books
- student-written materials

Effective language arts/English teachers recognize the importance of reading aloud well. They strive to constantly hone and refine this essential skill and may use audio- and video-taping as useful techniques in developing their readaloud abilities. They know that rehearsal is important.

Students should have the opportunity at times to respond to and reflect on a selection in their journals. Whatever the selection, many teachers ask for a written response only when they have a specific reason for doing so and only when the material lends itself to that kind of activity. Some days, teacher and students just share a "Wow!" after the reading and move on — anything else would be anti-climactic. Other days, the reading might stimulate some small-group discussion.

Too much writing can strangle a readaloud program.

After each readaloud, however, students can painlessly maintain the "tracking" function. They simply have to jot down the date and title of the readaloud selection in their response journals.

Teachers can explain what they're looking for in the way of response to readaloud and help cue the responses of those who need more support. The next student guideline, "Responding to a Readaloud," will assist teachers who are just getting started with response journals and want students to begin interacting with readalouds in a spontaneous and personally relevant manner.

If you've ever wondered about the value of reading picture books to older students, notice how Anthony Browne's *Piggybook* stimulates a highly sophisticated, philosophical "inner dialogue" in the following response by a 16-year-old student.

Response to Piggybook, *by Anthony Browne Readaloud, May 17*

When I realized that everything in the house was becoming pig-like, a little light bulb clicked on over my head. After the mother/wife left the house, whatever was inside the husband and children became more and more visible. Their

43

Responding to a Readaloud

When we listen to someone real aloud, our minds can be stimulated on a variety of levels. As we listen, we often jump quickly from idea to idea, image to image, or memory to memory. Sometimes, whatever we're thinking has been clearly stimulated by the reading. At other times, the link between what we're thinking and what we're listening to isn't immediately apparent.

After listening to this selection, try to describe what you were thinking about as you listened. Sometimes, you might be reminded of a similar, real or imagined incident; at other times, you might be especially impressed by the sound of the language or the feeling you get from a particular phrase. In reflecting on this selection, the place to start is your own personal reaction and how and why your mind reacted the way it did.

Some people have found the following kinds of questions useful in guiding their responses. These are only suggestions. Your own response to what you heard may not be covered by these questions.

- What were you thinking about?

- What kinds of images, feelings, or memories did the reading stimulate?

- What links can you trace between the reading and your thoughts?

- What was there about the reading that involved you the most?

- How were you interested or disappointed or surprised by what was read?

- What questions/comments come to mind?

- What springs to your mind that you want to ask about or say? (Don't worry about how "important" the detail or issue may be; if it's on your mind, it's important.)

physical transformation indicated the deep-rooted selfish, sexist, and mindless attitudes they had been carrying around inside.

Then I saw the wallpaper turn from flowers to pigs' heads and pigs' snouts and heads appeared everywhere from the doorknobs to the salt shaker. And then I started to wonder about how much we all turn the world into a reflection of what we are inside. Is the glass half-full or half-empty? But, if you're mean inside do you turn the world mean? Or does a mean world turn you mean? What about rose-colored glasses? Is it bad to live in a rosy world?

It's not as if we all can't agree that a door is a door. What I never really thought about before was how different we all feel about that door. Are we afraid of what's behind it? Anxious to open it? Is it locked all the time? It's like ten painters all painting the same scene and coming up with ten totally different versions of the same thing. Which is the real one? The one you painted or the one I painted?

Raymond (age 16)

A readaloud provides a common, public learning experience for discussion and reflection. We can observe how others react to the experience and compare and contrast our own reactions. While similar reactions can be shared and accepted with a look or nod of the head, differences need to be explored and resolved.

While reading aloud from *The Outsiders*, the teacher was moved to tears during the chapter describing Johnny's death. That reaction prompted an unusual student journal entry. As the student sketches his frustration, the response signals an issue that he has thought about before and that he will undoubtedly revisit.

Response to The Outsiders, *by S. E. Hinton Readaloud, Dec. 3*

I know this is going to sound sudden, but why did you cry? I know it was a very sad part but I don't really understand why people (don't worry, not just you) cry over books and movies. For one they are not real life and two it doesn't concern your life. I know this makes me seem insensitive but all people react in different ways (sorry).

Now that that's over with, I would like to say that you are a very good reader. I especially enjoy your voices. You make the book funny and exciting by the way you read. I think this book is O.K.

Jason (age 13)

Recently arrived from Kuwait, the next student had to make numerous adjustments. Although he had studied English in school, he was still operating in his second language. Used to a teacher-directed, autocratic classroom, he also had to grapple with his new responsibilities in an independent, personal response program.

The student showed some initiative, however. His teacher had been reading aloud Janet Lunn's *The Root Cellar*. Coincidentally, the teacher-librarian screened the video *Tom's Midnight Garden*, based on a novel by Philippa

Pearce. When asked to respond to that day's readaloud in his English class, the student chose without external direction to compare the two.

Notice how well the student makes connections. He displays a comprehensive understanding of the various plot lines and uses the related experience to confirm his judgments. Notice, as well, how clearly his meaning comes through in spite of his developing fluency.

Response to The Root Cellar, *by Janet Lunn Readaloud, pages 216–30, Jan. 30*

I like this part of the story because it is a very good way to end and show how things were getting, to solve who was Mrs. Morrissay, what had happened to Will and Susan, how did Rose make the Christmas dishes, and everything else otherwise.

It makes the ending look like <u>Tom's Midnight Garden</u> because in that Hattie was the old lady and in this story Susan was the old lady which Rose met when she came to Canada so mostly it is the same story. But a little change in the shape. Nice book.

Varun K. (age 12)

Response journals play a role in reading/writing conferences

By now, your students are responding not only to their own reading at school and at home but also to readalouds and, possibly, personal issues. Evaluating all this activity requires a palette of specific strategies and instruments, as outlined in Chapter 6. First, however, you need to find a way to keep track of what individuals are accomplishing from day to day, what their problems might be, and what you need to do to fine-tune your program.

Student/teacher conferences allow you to individualize your teaching, supervise individual progress, and adapt the program for specific needs. A conference will always work best when it's a collaborative effort between you and the student. As the recommendations that follow reflect, the student and the teacher share the responsibility for making the conference purposeful and productive.

Some teachers like to build as much flexibility into their conferences as possible. Rather than scheduling separate reading and writing conferences, they designate a time for a reading/writing conference. In this way, the purpose for the conference can be adapted to suit a student's needs and work pattern. Since many teachers have already implemented writing conferences as part of a writer's workshop approach to creative writing, the transition into dual-purpose conferences should be smooth.

Establish immediately that students automatically bring their response journals to any conference. When the conference, or part of it, is focused on the response journal, try to incorporate the following suggestions into your planning.

Focus on the purpose.

Build in continuity by starting with a review of the last conference and following up on any outstanding questions, tasks, or contracts arising from that conference.

Deal with the student's agenda next. A student might have a question arising from independent reading, a problem encountered in a small-group discussion,

46

or any number of other concerns. If you demonstrate that you respect and value the students' agendas, they will develop self-direction and their agendas will grow and flourish.

With your own agenda, maintain objectivity and keep value judgments to a minimum. The conference should be an exchange of views and a problem-solving discussion, not a "third-degree." For example, you may be concerned about the small amount of material being read. If you start off by advising students that they're not reading enough, you set up an adversarial tone right away and effectively short-circuit the conference's problem-solving potential. Instead, ask the students to describe how much they're reading, how this amount compares with their normal rate, what difficulties they may be encountering with the material, or what may be preoccupying them.

Depending on what you discover, you may feel the reading effort is adequate or you may want to establish a contract to increase the amount read. If so, make sure you have the students set realistic goals over a reasonably short period of time and decide how and when progress toward those goals will be reviewed.

Conferences are an ideal setting for one-to-one remediation. You might notice, for instance, that a student is retelling in most responses and you want to extend their response repertoire. During the conference, you can suggest more variety, indicate another type of response, and describe how the student might introduce it in their current reading. Again, set a specific, realistic goal, such as introducing a different kind of response for every second or third entry.

Conferences are also custom made for setting individual reading goals. Some of your students read one or more novels at home each evening; some read only whatever they read in school. Some are fluent readers; others are reluctant readers. Some students have learning exceptionalities that block their understanding. Many students have English as their first language; others have just transferred into your class from an English as a Second Language program.

All students need feasible goals consistent with their capabilities and developing stages of fluency. One size won't fit all. Talk to individuals about their reading histories. Agree in the conference on the amount of reading that each student might fairly and productively accomplish over a specific period of time and ask the student to record that goal in the student's journal.

Encourage reflective thinking.

As a record of a process over time, the response journal supplies you with a number of checkpoints in a variety of areas. By linking a specific set of checkpoints, you and the student can discuss the profile that takes shape. For example, you may have noted a student's reluctance to support opinions with proof from the text. By mentioning this observation and checking through the response journal records, you and the student can place the observation in a context over time and assess its validity.

Similarly, other patterns revealed in the response journals need to be identified, discussed, and evaluated. Possible patterns include dependency on a certain type of response, a disinclination to stray beyond the cueing questions, and a tendency toward the glib or superficial. Encourage students to take a critical approach to their own responses and to make doing so a prime objective.

Growth in self-evaluation and independence in learning go hand in hand with and develop out of reflection.

Ask genuine questions.

Many books on writing and reading conferences contain lists of the kinds of questions you should be asking. Actually, you are already perfectly capable of asking any question you need to ask. The key is to make sure you really want to find out the answer.

Try not to ask questions to which you already know the answers. Through so much exposure to these kinds of questions over the years, students instantly realize that these questions signal a "test." Why else would someone ask a question when he or she already knows the answer? The student, then, tries to guess the "right" answer in your mind. When you ask that kind of question, the collaborative, problem-solving tone of the conference is lost.

Instead, try to respond to the student as you would to a peer. If you're confused, say so. Then ask whatever questions are necessary to clear up the confusion. If you think something may be bothering the student, say so. Explain why you think that way and ask the student to clarify the situation for you. If you have a reason to probe, probe. If you and the student have nothing further to say, the conference is over.

Try to pursue a more interesting line than asking students to "tell" you about the latest book they have read. If they're reading science fiction, for example, find out if you and the student have read some of the same books or watched similar science-fiction films or television shows. Then explore your common experiences and see how the new book fits in. You thereby avoid a long and tedious retelling.

Ask students, as well, to place specific experiences into a larger context, synthesize a variety of print and media experiences, or reflect on why and how they read the way they do. Entries in the student's response journal on readalouds or remarks and observations about a film, for example, can raise intriguing questions. The discussions should be a learning experience for both of you. Follow your own instincts, react naturally and spontaneously, and always try to hold up your end of a real discussion.

Set definite time limits. With large classes, it's important to keep the conferences functional; make sure that you're accomplishing meaningful tasks with each one. Beware of working your way through the class out of a sense of duty. Unless you organize your conferences carefully and remain flexible and selective in your approach, you'll soon feel as though you're trapped on a giant gerbil wheel, running flat out just to stay in one place.

Establish a "do-able" routine; if you have time to sit down with each student only once every two weeks, then so be it. Set a maximum time for each conference, let the student know, and observe the limits. If you haven't covered everything, either leave the other issues until the next time or schedule another conference.

The response journals will work best if they are reviewed regularly face to face. Set a schedule and stick with it. As well, there's no minimum time. When the student's agenda and your own have been covered, the conference is over.

Keep records. At the very least, both you and the student should record that the conference took place on a specific date. The student should note this and any other information related to the conference in a response journal.

Any other record-keeping should be purposeful. For example, if you and the student agree to meet in two days' time, both of you should make a note of it. If you've given the student a specific task or suggestion, ask the student to jot it down. If you're going to try to locate a specific book for a student, write down the title in your records. (See the sample record-keeping sheet, page 49).

Sample Conference Record-Keeping

The following sample gives you an idea of the shape teacher record-keeping might take and the course of entries over a month.

Student Name: Wilson, Sean

Conference date	Issues /Observations / Actions / Goals
Sept. 7	- first conference; reads mostly sports and wrestling magazines outside school; watches sitcoms, wrestling, music videos on T.V. - will help him pick out a novel
Sept. 13	- has started and discarded several suggested novels; says they're "boring"; is "tracking" in journal, but no responses; wants to bring magazines to class - will try high interest/appropriate vocabulary material (_The Last War_); have agreed on a goal of 2 responses per week
Sept. 20	- about 1/3 into _Last War_; wonders why some people died and some didn't; predicts boy and girl will fall in love and start a new human race - has written 2 brief responses since last conference, both "retelling"
Sept. 28	- finished _Last War_; surprised girl died; asked what happens to boy; pointed out clues to him from text; talked about meaning of ending - journal entries "retelling," but some personal reactions ("cool" parts, surprise and disappointment at ending) - needs another book; willing to try other books in same series; will pick one out today

Although the conference itself should not be evaluated, you should note certain kinds of details. For example, if agreement is reached on an issue or an unusual observation comes out of the conference, you would want to write it down. You would definitely want to record the fact when a student agrees to read more and how this goal will be achieved. By the same token, if a student makes a shrewd analogy during the conference, revealing a new interest, a sudden insight, or a lot of extracurricular reading, you'd want to note those observations, too.

For record purposes, one page per student per term is convenient and workable. Any less and you wouldn't have enough space to make your notes; any more and you might say too much and get lost in the paperwork. Many teachers like to keep the pages in a small, loose-leaf binder.

Post-it notes are a handy way of recording observations between conferences. Just write the observation, date it, and stick it on the student's page. When the conference comes up, you can discuss the observation with the student and, if appropriate, make a permanent record of it.

The record-keeping should hold no secrets or surprises for anyone. Students should always know what you are recording, why you are recording that information, and how it might enter into their evaluation.

Teachers can empower students through personal response

The explanations, directions, and guidelines in this chapter provide the structure for implementing and maintaining a personal response program. The ultimate success of the program, however, rests on the knowledge, skills and judgment of the classroom teacher.

The old adage that a love of reading is caught, not taught still rings true and applies equally well to a love of literature. Teachers who can transmit a personal sense of excitement and wonder about a piece of writing, such as a poem, picture book, or short story, and articulate their own idiosyncratic web of related thoughts, feelings, and memories impart to students an immediate and irreplaceable model of the power of personal response.

The suggestions in this chapter operate most effectively when regarded as a palette from which teachers choose, apply, and supplement as the needs of their students warrant. A flourishing personal response program requires teachers to constantly monitor their students' progress and intervene when necessary in innumerable ways each day. A teacher might have to sit down with an individual student, for example, and illustrate how to fashion an effective written response to a particular story from one of the cueing questions. Another student might be churning out response after response with little reflection or insight; the teacher might need to wean that student away from a strict reliance on cueing questions and into formulating self-generated and more personally satisfying questions and comments. The teacher might help another student find an appropriate independent reading selection and engage still another student in a discussion of a controversial issue arising from a journal entry.

In a successful personal response program, the teacher is neither the "sage on the stage" nor the "guide on the side" but rather a little of both and everything in between. In a variety of roles and in a thousand and one different ways, teachers empower their students through personal response to discover their own voices and take control of and accept responsibility for their own learning.

50

4

Responding to live and mass media

The application of response journals extends far beyond reading and literature programs into the full range of media events. Media, in the larger sense, refers to the many means of communicating and processing thoughts, such as newspapers, magazines, film, television, and live theatre. Whenever students seek to discover and explain the stated and unstated meanings in the vicarious experiences that influence their lives, from exploring and analyzing the impact of a live theatre performance to deconstructing the techniques, jargon, and images of print and electronic advertising, response journals have a role to play.

Writing-in-role builds upon drama in education

Response journals can serve drama in education programs. Drama as a learning/ teaching technique involves students in spontaneous, unscripted activities without an audience. Role-playing, whereby students explore the thoughts and feelings of another by behaving and responding as that person, is central to it. Drama in education helps students explore, make connections among, and learn about the issues, events, and relationships that affect their lives.

Beyond playing roles, students can write in role. Response journals allow students to assume the personae of fictional characters or real-life people and explore issues by writing through another's eyes. Writing-in-role has a host of applications, from enriching a character study in English class to examining a historical event from a broad range of perspectives. Teachers who employ this evocative technique will discover response journals to be the ideal medium for creating and collecting these written exercises in role-playing.

The subject for the following writing-in-role arose during a discussion of conservation in a science class. In groups of four or five, the students brainstormed lists of issues they felt needed to be addressed. They then focused on one of the issues and discussed problems and possible solutions. One group entered into a heated debate on whaling that carried on into their English class. The teacher recommended that the members of the group turn to their response journals and attempt to clarify why they were each so stirred by the issue. Since emotions were so high, the teacher suggested writing-in-role as one technique for exploring their feelings.

While the direct identification with the young animal in this narrative is vividly realized, the emotional content and balance of the piece as a whole is especially striking. Through writing-in-role, the student transforms the issue from an abstract event into a clearly articulated, personal tragedy.

Responding by writing-in-role, April 21

We swim peacefully through the still water, playing happily in the sun-touched waters. Mother and I surface for a breath of fresh air. As we swim back down, we hear noises coming from the world above. They startle us and we swim as fast as we can towards the bottom, Mother shielding me with her body. Hoping we're far enough down, we turn to look back.

A large platform floats above us. Suddenly, a large net plunges into the water. Mother swerves to avoid it, but instead she snags herself in it. She thrashes and struggles, screaming at me to run. I move closer. I cry out to her, but I have to back off as the net and Mother slowly disappear into the world above. My shrill squeaking cries are lost in the turmoil. Then the net plunges again. I swerve and swim as fast as I can and just miss getting caught. When I turn again, the net is gone. I look up and the platform is moving now, heading towards land. Numbly, I follow.

I swim for a long time before the platform reaches land. I carefully surface to have a look. I see Mother lying helplessly at the mercy of four men with large sticks with sharp, pointed ends. They bring their arms up. Then they send the sticks crashing down deep into her body. I hear her yelp and gasp with pain. She gives one last flick of her tail and her eyes close. A stream of blood runs down her body.

Stunned, I sink into the water and swim alone to the bottom of the sea and think of Mother and fear the day they will come again, for me.

Cindy (age 14)

The impact of theatre prompts reflection

Performance drama possesses a unique and potent immediacy and intimacy that no other medium can match. Printed material requires students to actively conjure characters and situations from their imaginations, while film and television, however starkly and realistically presented, are always physically at a remove from the audience and fabricated in bits and pieces until a workable representation is constructed. When a book is closed or a video turned off, the fictional world disappears. No such barriers, real or imagined, separate an audience from a stage production. The people on stage breathe and move in the same time and space as the members of the audience. This startling immediacy imbues their performances with unparalleled realism, force, and conviction.

The next student guideline, "Responding to a Stage Production," underscores the unique features of live productions and offers suggestions for responding in writing to this kind of presentation.

Student Guideline

Responding to a Stage Production

A stage production tells a story in a totally different way from a film or a television program. In a stage production, for example, the audience and the actors are in the same place at the same time and remain there together as long as it takes for the story to be told. While a scene for a film or video can be shot over and over again, edited after the shooting, and augmented by reality-altering special effects, a stage production unfolds from beginning to end right in front of your eyes with no opportunity for retakes. As you watch a live theatre production, however, none of these differences will affect your understanding or enjoyment. On the contrary, you'll discover yourself drawn into the make-believe world in ways you scarcely expect.

Once you've seen a performance, first describe, in your journals, those moments when you reacted to whatever was happening on stage with some kind of emotion, such as surprise, fear, laughter, anger, disappointment, approval, or disapproval, and try to determine why you felt that way. Don't worry about retelling the story or talking about the play in sequence from the beginning. Instead, express your strongest impressions of the play as they occur to you.

You may want to discuss some of the following elements of the stage production and their impact on you. Remember that these are only suggestions.

- How did the actors use spoken language, their voices, their gestures, or their body language to convey who the characters were and how they were feeling? Which characters were most memorable and why?

- Think about the way the actors entered, exited, and moved about the stage. How did any of this staging reinforce the storytelling?

- How did the lighting contribute to the mood or enhance the telling of the story?

- How did the music, if any, contribute to the mood or strengthen the performance?

- How were sound effects, if any, used in the play and how did they add to the telling of the story?

- What events or ideas from the play seemed important to you or stand out in your mind?

- How did the scenery, costumes, and props add to the storytelling?

An intermediate student recorded her reactions to a play called "More Than Words." The play was written and performed by a group of drama students from a neighboring secondary school. The students had devised a series of vignettes based on their own school experiences. Since the play had been commissioned by the local board of education to support the introduction of its new anti-harassment policy, the subject of the play was sexual harassment.

The intermediate audience was only a few months away from entering that secondary school, so the play had added personal significance for them. Notice especially in this entry how the student uses her own experiences as a female as an entry point to understanding and sympathizing with the victims of homophobia. She realized that the victims of sexism and homophobia have something in common and correctly perceived gay rights to be an equity issue.

Response to the play, "More Than Words," April 22

I enjoyed this play a lot. I felt it was very realistic and it definitely seemed like a real day in a high school. I thought the language they used like the slang and swearing and all was necessary to make it realistic but there wasn't too much of it. The play dealt with many important issues such as sexual and verbal harassment and gay rights and feelings. It was exactly what we talked about the day before in class.

I thought the most powerful scene was when the two girls were at each side of the stage and talked about how they felt. The emotions they showed on their faces had the feelings of anger and pain all mixed together. I thought the boy was so manipulative the way he was conning her to think it was all her fault. No wonder women always feel like the weaker ones if everyone is always shutting you off. How can you feel safe to tell someone so that they will believe you?

Sexual harassment is really mean and getting pleasure from putting someone down is not right. I also think discrimination against gays and lesbians is stupid. They are just normal people like us who have sexual feelings for the same sex. People are always using putdowns like "fag" and "lezzie" and you can't say anything or they'll call that to you. It's like they don't have anybody.

All these things I pointed out were expressed very well in the play. I really enjoyed watching this play. It really taught me a lot about sexual harassment and letting us see a day of school next year. I am glad that I learned but I hope people outside will learn that it is not right and it shouldn't be happening.

Donna (age 13)

Responding to media helps foster awareness of values

Media experiences possess potential for both insight and distortion.

In its positive form, a media experience can touch us emotionally and intellectually, stimulate reflection, and encourage inner change. An artist's vision can help us illuminate, reassess, and possibly redirect what we believe, what we value, and how we conduct our lives.

Conversely, a media experience can also negatively reconstruct our vision of reality. Media representations can be accepted too literally. With films, television, videotape, and electronic and print advertising, the image seems so "real" that we accept the persuasive, attractive, and powerful image as truth. If that "truth" is riddled with a variety of stereotypes or with an unbalanced or extreme view of sexuality or violence, then the image tends to reinforce our own negative values.

Some people see that link as a reason for censorship, but in so doing, they fail to recognize that values run both ways. As with reading print, comprehension of media occurs in the mind and is directly affected by an individual's experiences and values. Depending on past experiences and the beliefs and values developed from those experiences, two people can witness the same image and come away with two totally different perceptions. A stereotype, for instance, appears on the screen. Whether the viewer "sees" that stereotype as "good" or "bad," however, depends not on the screen image but rather on a viewer's personal value system. Censoring media does nothing to change those perceptions.

The place to initiate change is with an individual's *perception* of an image, not with the image itself. Helping students deconstruct and analyze media experiences fosters awareness and understanding. Recognizing how a media event operates is the first step in breaking its hold on the unconscious. Instead of burying media stereotypes, we need to bring them out into the light of day.

Personal response to media is crucial to the process of uncovering and coming to terms with our operational values. For change to occur, an individual needs to first identify the value system influencing a particular perception. Only then can the person reflect on and start to understand why the experience is perceived in that way. The values underlying the perception can then be tested in a variety of contexts.

During the personal response process, teachers shouldn't expect to see light bulbs of total understanding pop on over their students' heads. Although sudden moments of insight and enlightenment occur, media literacy usually unfolds gradually with time, repeated exposure, and opportunities to deconstruct and reflect on media language. As such, personal response is one component of an integrated unit affording opportunities to read and view, write and represent, and discuss and reflect.

Always begin exploring students' personal responses to media with the media and messages to which they are most exposed and susceptible. Next, devise as many in-class opportunities as possible for them to view, respond to, and discuss each type of experience. Although some techniques are common from one medium to another, keep in mind that each medium is a separate entity with a separate language and a separate set of rules governing its operation.

Students need to start with their own experiences and build outward. An awareness of technique or general patterns will unfold gradually. Too much adult input too soon can be counterproductive; lists of media techniques and specialized jargon can be off-putting or confusing.

The process of recording their responses to a wide range of media experiences will help students, first, to codify them and, later, to facilitate analysis and understanding. As with anything worthwhile and important, the process takes time, but can be illuminating.

Students can investigate TV's impact

The statistics derived from television's looming presence have become almost commonplace. We're no longer shocked by the fact that high school graduates have been exposed to hundreds of hours of television commercials, or that they've spent less time in school than watching television. While we're uneasy about the content of much that appears on television, we're not sure what to do about it.

The popularity of specialty cable channels, the Internet, gaming modules, and home video, moreover, has fragmented television's audience and encouraged an "edgier" approach to programming. As networks vie for viewers with increasingly salacious, violent, and controversial programs, we accept the vagaries and questionable content of programming fads as inevitable and immutable.

In spite of these electronic facts of life, however, we remain unsure of the impact this kind of exposure is having on our students' value systems, or even our own. From the cartoon-like stereotypes of sitcoms to the glossy and romanticized violence of crime shows, television presents an endless barrage of aberrated images. When a rapid-fire, highly edited, and carefully managed newscast is blithely accepted as a realistic portrayal of day-to-day events, where do students draw the line?

How much of what our students see on television do they accept as "real" and how able are they to see through what they view?

The main difficulty in dealing with television programming in schools is the lack of immediacy. We want our students to develop an interactive relationship with a medium that appears temptingly benign and passive. Except for educational programming, however, their viewing habits are developed and maintained in their homes.

To bridge the actual experience of viewing and the processing of that experience through discussion and reflection, students need to become aware of and examine their personal relationship with television. Through their response journals, students can investigate television's impact. They can examine what they watch, how they're being touched by what they watch, and why they continue to watch.

First, however, the teacher and students need a clear picture of what everyone is watching and how often. Students need to become aware of their own viewing habits and those of their friends.

The survey "Who's Watching What?" can begin the process. Ask students to fill out the chart individually. Next, gather the data from the class using an overhead of the "Who's Watching What? Data Collection" page. Provide each student with a copy of this checklist as well. As you go through the types of programs, tell students to raise their hands whenever they've checked a particular type. They should note the daily and weekly totals on their own copies of the Data Collection page for future reference. Once you've filled in this page, move on to the student guideline, "Responding to 'Who's Watching What?'"

Be sure to emphasize that viewing habits vary considerably. Some students watch little or no television on weekdays, for example, while others don't watch television at all. Beyond checking the "no" category on the initial "Who's Watching What?" survey, these students will not see their lives reflected in the data collection. Suggest that these students keep track in their journals of their own daily, recreational activities and use this record to compare how they spend their time with the time many of their peers spend watching television or videos.

Who's Watching What?

This survey will help you examine your viewing habits over a seven-day period. Think back over the last week or over a typical viewing week and decide how often you watch the following types of programs. If you watch a particular kind of show every day for seven days, check it off each day. (If you watch that type of program more than once a day, still just count it as "once.") Count only the viewing you do outside of school.

Type of Program	Daily Totals							Totals	
	Mon.	Tues.	Wed.	Thurs.	Fri.	Sat.	Sun.	Me	Class
Cartoons									
Comedy/Variety									
Game shows									
Talk shows									
Sitcoms									
Sports									
Daytime "soaps"									
"Reality" shows									
Drama									
Crime/Adventure									
Hospital/Legal									
Fantasy/Sci-Fi									
News									
Nature & Outdoor									
TV movies									
Movies on video									
Music channels									
No television or movies									
Other (Please list)									

Teacher/Student Checklist

Who's Watching What?

Data Collection

Record daily and weekly totals once numbers are determined through a show of hands called for by the teacher.

Type of Program	Daily Totals							Weekly Totals
	Mon.	Tues.	Wed.	Thurs.	Fri.	Sat.	Sun.	
Cartoons								
Comedy/Variety								
Game shows								
Talk shows								
Sitcoms								
Sports								
Daytime "soaps"								
"Reality" shows								
Drama								
Crime/Adventure								
Hospital/Legal								
Fantasy/Sci-Fi								
News								
Nature & Outdoor								
TV movies								
Movies on video								
Music channels								
No television or movies								
Other (Please list)								

Student Guideline

Responding to "Who's Watching What?"

The viewing survey "Who's Watching What?" gives you a profile of your own viewing habits and the viewing habits of your class. In your journal, comment on those results, the impressions you gained from the profile, and what you've learned about yourself and TV watching. The following questions may serve as a springboard into your feelings on the matter. You don't have to answer every question. You're free to talk about your thoughts and reactions your own way.

- How does your own profile compare with that of the class? How are your viewing habits the same or different?

- What aspects of your viewing habits surprised you or made you feel uneasy or embarrassed? Why?

- What aspects of other people's viewing habits surprised you? What have you learned about other people from these results?

- What impressed you about the results or what seemed especially significant to you?

- What picture of you as a television watcher emerges from the survey? How does this picture compare with how you regard yourself or what you thought before taking the survey?

- What more would you like to know about your own viewing habits or those of your friends? Why?

Once students have discussed, analyzed, and reflected on the results of the viewing surveys, they're ready to focus on specific categories. Guidelines for eliciting personal responses to some of the more popular television genres follow. The order in which you deal with these categories or how many of them you include in your media literacy unit will depend on the survey results and your own reading of your class's needs.

Recognize differences in media experiences.

Students who watch little or no television have no context for completing the media activities involving "soaps," sitcoms, and TV advertising. Some students may also have little exposure to adolescent magazines when print advertising is examined. As well, students who do have experience with all these forms of media may be interested in investigating one aspect more than another. The activities are meant to stimulate interest in and focus attention on the social and cultural influences that shape our values, attitudes, and behavior. The goal is to channel this ongoing cycle of investigation, reflection, and problem-solving back into the independent response journal process, *not* cover all the activities in the unit. For these reasons, teachers should consider setting up interest groups when implementing this section. After the groups have contemplated their activities, volunteers from each group can present their discoveries and insights to the whole class.

Students can choose among the following activities:

- "soaps" and sitcoms (page 61)
- TV advertising (page 63)
- print advertising (page 65)

The more resources at hand in the classroom the better. During the examination of print advertising, students can augment the magazine collections found in school libraries with magazines brought in from home. For TV advertising, compilations of prize-winning commercials are readily available from school video catalogues and from public libraries. Student volunteers are also delighted to videotape a selection of commercials for use in the classroom. Students without these resources can use them in the classroom or library or teachers may prefer to use some of them with the class as a whole.

What's real about "soaps" and sitcoms?

Two of the most popular types of programs on television use an exaggerated and distorted form of reality to great effect. Both count on developing loyal fans who will watch their programs regularly over a long period of time. Both contain the potential for bending our expectations for the lives we lead.

With daytime "soaps," action is slowed down to such an extent that events seem to unfold at the same rate they do in real life. A crisis, for example, drags on over a number of episodes and characters agonize over each developing detail much as "real" people might. Small wonder that with action at a minimum and crisis at the maximum the world of soaps is awash with emotions.

In this highly charged, emotional context, the pull to identify with the physically attractive and primarily youthful characters is strong and insidious. The combination of struggling, romantic figures and gritty, seamy, outrageous, or improbable situations is almost irresistible.

60

Student Guideline

Responding to "Soaps" and Sitcoms

Think of your favorite "soaps" or sitcoms (or the ones you watch the most). Week after week, certain features about the shows attract you. Sometimes, memorable episodes dealing with a specific issue in a particular way will draw you in especially. Perhaps something about one character really appeals to you. Probably for a combination of reasons, the characters and situations have gained your attention and will continue to do so.

Consider these programs in general and certain favorite episodes in particular. What thoughts and feelings arise immediately and remain uppermost in your mind? What can you learn about yourself by looking at your attraction to these programs? It you have difficulty unravelling your thoughts and feelings about this issue, some of the following questions may trigger a significant response.

- How do you explain your attraction and loyalty to a particular show?

- What strong opinions or reactions have been stirred up in you by what the characters do or say? What do your reactions tell you about yourself?

- With whom do you identify most closely on this particular show? Least closely?

- How are these people like or unlike you or who you want to be?

- How do these characters compare with the people you meet every day?

- If you could have characters from the show live in your real world, who would you choose? Why? How would real life be affected by these changes?

- If you could have real people you know live in the world of the television show, who would you choose? Why? How would the world of the television show be changed?

61

Night-time "soups" or other dramatic series duplicate the same formula weekly instead of daily. Since their emotions are just like ours, we can identify with the rich and powerful regardless of our socio-economic status. Even when the characters are incredibly privileged, accomplished, or powerful, we still respond to their plight. For good or bad, the bridge between their world and ours is easily negotiated. We recognize, we identify with, and we're moved.

With sitcoms (situation comedies), the context comes first. Characters may be stereotypical and their behavior often bizarre, but we can validate their long-term relationships and the familiar and predictable problems they encounter. In spite of the fact that the characters, their reactions, and their approaches to the resolution of conflict are exaggerated, oversimplified, and frequently irrational, we recognize, we identify with, and we laugh.

The danger is that we accept the concerns, attitudes, aspirations, and values we see as real. If students see television as a window into the functioning of the actual world or as a standard against which to judge their own lives, they will be confused and unhappy. By recording their personal responses in a journal, students can begin to crystallize and articulate what kind of sense they're making of these television "realities" and why they're making that kind of sense.

Let students explore the role of advertising

Television viewing has become such an intrinsic part of our society that we often lose sight of the dynamics that propel the medium. Under the constant onslaught of images, we tend to passively endure rather than actively analyze. Yet advertising has a huge impact. If a commercial catches our attention with a slogan or catch-phrase, we even become part of the process by integrating the "sound bite" into our daily lives. If we see a brand-new car racing around a hairpin turn with ease or an attractive model using a particular product, we're apt to think, "Hmmm. Looks good!" We know better, but the selling process insidiously pulls us in; if it happens unconsciously, that's even better.

Students are more emotionally and intellectually vulnerable to the myriad sales techniques than most adults. At the same time that they have more exposure to advertising, they possess less awareness of the selling dynamic and fewer analytical tools to combat the persuasive messages.

Personal response enables students to take an individually significant route into the maze-like world of advertising and to expose and explain the techniques of manipulation and persuasion. The temptation during media literacy units, however, is to short-circuit the discovery process and tell too much too soon. The knowledge that teachers possess about advertising and want to pass on will take root more effectively after students explore the role that advertising has in their lives and mull over what they make of it all. Besides, even though they may not be aware of it, students already have an enormous reservoir of information about advertising. They just need a way to tap that reservoir.

The next guideline, "Responding to TV Advertising," sparks personal responses based on students' existing knowledge and encourages initial reflection on some of the underlying issues.

Student Guideline

Responding to TV Advertising

Television commercials are designed to persuade. Advertisers hire agencies to invent sure-fire ways to persuade a particular viewer or reader to buy a particular product or service or to agree with a particular point of view.

Have you ever watched a commercial on television and wondered how such a silly or strange or obvious image could possibly be effective? Appearances can be deceiving. More likely than not, the message wasn't meant for you. All advertising is carefully researched and crafted to sell someone something.

Sometimes, advertisers want a particular group of people merely to remember a name or a slogan or recognize a package. Sometimes, they're trying to convince you that you must have that product or service. Keep in mind that advertisers will spend millions of dollars to create and preview a 30-second commercial during the Super Bowl. Let the buyer beware!

Think about a television commercial that you especially like or dislike. Briefly describe that commercial or ad. Discuss your reactions to it and why you think it has that effect. Write in your journal about whatever comes to mind as you reflect on the images and the messages. If you're not sure what to write about, the following questions will get you started. Answer some or none of them, depending on how much you have to say about the topic in your own way.

- What is it about the commercial that attracts or repels you? What is the advertiser trying to get you to do? How are you being convinced to do that? How does the world of the commercial compare with your own life?
- As you think about the commercial, what images come to mind? What colors, pictures, words or slogans, actions, or simple stories linger in your mind? Why would these elements impress you? What connection can you make between these elements and your own life, likes, and dislikes?
- What are some of the techniques or images in this commercial that remind you of other commercials? What do they tell you about yourself and your own needs and dreams? Why would advertisers keep using these techniques and images?
- What connections, if any, can you find between the kind of television show and the content and nature of the advertising? What other patterns have you noticed in terms of where and when commercials are placed? What kinds of products or services are sold during your favorite television programs? Why might that be?
- Many commercials are designed to have an appeal for or an effect on a particular group of people. Other groups of people might ignore or tune out the advertising. What was the target group for this commercial? What is it about the commercial that will attract or convince this target group? Why do these techniques work on this group of people? What would advertisers say about the group you belong to?

How does print advertising make us feel?

While the viewer profile "Who's Watching What?" demonstrates the all-pervasive presence of television, specialty magazines also occupy a significant niche in students' lives. Advertisers avidly target fashion, fan, video game, and sports magazines, among others, that cater to the special interests of student buyers. Both magazines and TV use similar selling tactics.

Help students become further aware of advertising techniques. Ask your students to collect five or six print advertisements preferably from magazines and newspapers they have been reading. Some samples should be in color. They can initially work with "Responding to a Print Ad" (next page).

Try to focus your students before they begin.

Remind your students that when we look at an ad, our minds are active on a variety of levels. Although we are not consciously aware of what's happening, our eyes quickly dart from feature to feature all over the page. In that split second, our minds are interconnecting colors with feelings with images with feelings with memories with feelings, and so on. Trying to trace those connections is next to impossible.

If we are part of the group targeted for that ad, we are supposed to feel a certain way about it. Remind the students that how they feel is the place to start. Then ask them to look over the ads they have collected, thinking only of how they feel about them. Tell them to choose the one that is most appealing, intriguing, or powerful.

In her response to a print ad for Covergirl eyeliner and lip color, this young student follows her subjective reactions to some unsettling questions about her world. The ad appeared in a teen fashion magazine.

Response to a print ad
May 11

It's funny that when I was flipping through the magazine looking at the ads and not the articles, I was able to see different things. Like most of the ads had white women, usually blonde, but they had a few ads at the beginning with women of color in them. I guess most of the people who buy the magazine are white people except if you're black and you just look at the first few pages you might buy it because you see black women there in the ads.

Anyway, it was amazing in this one ad that the whole page was mostly this blonde's face staring out and with her shoulders showing. She had her hair around her face like a lion's mane or something and even her skin was blonde and the background was white and the little bit of her dress you could see was white. So, it's a white person's ad.

The slogan on the ad is "Color Me Smooth." That goes along with everything in the ad, like her hair and her skin and her face are all smooth and shiny. Just like we talked about she looks perfect and unreal. You can really notice her eyes and the color of her lips because the colors stand out against all that blonde and white. It's funny, too, that the black models in the other ads look smooth and thin and perfect just like the blonde models.

If guys saw these models they'd be like, "wow," and it's hard to look good like those models. I guess the ad is saying that if you want to look good to guys you

64

Responding to a Print Ad

As you look more closely at the advertisement you've chosen, try to describe the kind of impression you've formed of it, the features you notice, or the thoughts or memories or emotions connected with it that you can identify.

What do you notice about how your mind is reacting? Don't try to "understand" the ad. Let your eyes rest on the page. Be aware of colors, patterns, shapes, images, words or phrases, and the total "look."

Some students have found the following kinds of questions useful in guiding their responses. These questions are prompts only. Follow and trust your own reactions, thoughts, and feelings.

- What aspects of the ad seem to draw your attention? How do they make you feel?

- What connections do you start to make between the ad and your own life, the way it is now or the way you would like it to be? How does the ad seem to stimulate your dreams, your desires, or your fears?

- What flashes of memory surface as you consider the ad? What feelings (e.g., embarrassment, humiliation, excitement, guilt, fear) are identified with these episodes? How did the ad make these memories surface?

- Try to enter the world of the advertisement. If that world were merged with your own, what parts of the advertisement world would have to change in order to become real and truly fit in with your life? What aspects of your life could realistically change to become more like the world of the ad?

should use those products. But I wonder if people want to be like that or if the ads make them want to be like that. What do you think?

Stacey (age 14)

Students need to get past first impressions with film

A personal response to a film often operates in a different manner from a response to reading a book or story. Film is a mixture of sound, motion, and picture. The "reality" of the film is so vividly and fully realized that the mind becomes involved in vicariously living that reality and less consciously reflective of the experience.

Upon immediate reflection, many students feel that a film "was what it was." They liked it or they didn't like it; they liked some of the characters or they didn't. Usually they have a difficult time removing themselves from the film in an objective way. Since a film is often a less obvious "construction" than a novel or a music video, it's easier to accept an impression rather than probe the feelings behind that impression. In a sense, the experience is too "real" to analyze or question.

The next student guideline, "Responding to a Film," can be used with any film or video. The questions encourage students to trace the connections between what they've viewed and their own lives prior to analyzing their reactions. Teachers might consider employing the guideline with a film screened in class. The different responses to an identical experience would stimulate fruitful discussion and further insight.

In one instance, a teacher showed a film on the image of women in advertising. The intent was to help students get beyond the surface impact of ads and begin to appreciate the deliberate constructions. In the process, the teacher hoped to provide students with some of the visual language of ads and stimulate discussion of stereotyping and embedded values. As the following response indicates, the film offers some powerful and provocative images.

Response to the film Still Killing Us Softly,* *Oct. 21*

It's hard not to feel angry and kind of sick when you see how women are trapped in this image and everyone thinks it's just fine. So maybe there are two sides and guys are trapped in this macho thing too. But they aren't packaged up and told that growing old is bad and how dumb they are and treated like an idiot toy and turned against each other.

But what's frightening is that it all happens so naturally and it all seems so right. You see the ads and the TV commercials and you know that it's all around you all the time. And everybody talks about how sexism is so bad and your parents and your teachers and the government tell you you can be anything you want but do you see women as principals much or as heads of companies or in the government?

The worst thing is that if you don't want to be a house-keeper or a baby machine you have to turn into a man to get ahead in the business world! How do you get people to change? You look at the television programs and rock videos and you know that no matter what some people are saying nothing is really different.

**Still Killing Us Softly: Advertising's Image of Women. Cambridge Documentary Films.

66

Student Guideline

Responding to a Film

Think about a film you've seen. Don't worry about retelling the story or even talking about whether it was "good" or "bad." Try, instead, to think about you and your life in connection with the film and the characters in it.

- What connections are you making?
- What personal feelings or memories are surfacing?
- What seems important about the film that you want to say?

If what you want to say about the film isn't clear, reflect on some of the following questions. Remember that these are only suggestions.

- When you think about this film, what first comes to your mind? Is there an image or character or situation that you start to think about? Why do think that is?
- Do you start to think about the film by remembering a gesture someone made or a dominant color you noticed, a controversial issue, or, perhaps, something that confused you? Where do these thoughts lead? What connection, if any, do your impressions have with your own life?
- What startling/unsettling/vivid images seem to stick in your mind? What is it that you remember about these images or the way they were presented? How do they seem to tie in with the experiences or feelings you've had in real life?
- Does a character, a situation, or an issue in the film remind you of the real world or your own life? How do they compare? How does the real-life experience affect what you think about the screen experience? How does the screen experience affect your understanding of the real-life experience?
- Do you wish your own life or the people you know were more like the world of the film and the characters in that world? Did you identify with one character more than any other? What was it about that character that appealed to you?
- How much did you agree or disagree with the people in the film, the way they behaved, or the kinds of values and beliefs they displayed? Explain your feelings and your point of view.

Maybe it's even more frightening. People want us to believe that there is no longer a problem. Well, guess again! Open a magazine. Turn on the TV. Talk to your boy friend!

Wanda K. (age 15)

Newspapers and magazines raise issues for response

Newspapers and magazines of all types can and should be brought into the classroom for reading and study. Special attention should be paid to the ones that students read, the sections they favor, and the issues and stories that attract them most. Eventually, in any long-term and comprehensive media literacy unit, students will learn how and why to discriminate among newspapers and magazines. The first step in this process is to help them reflect on what they're reading and why.

For the following activity, students should have both newspapers and magazines and the time to flip through them and read whatever attracts them. Ideally, a variety of materials should be available to satisfy whatever style of reporting individuals prefer. Most teachers prefer to separate the study of the newspaper from that of the magazine. The next student guideline, "Responding to Newspapers," offers questions to prompt reflection.

The response below originated in a Grade 8 classroom. The students had been following newspaper articles on a couple who had killed their child who had severe disabilities. The controversial case agitated and dismayed them, and they had discussed the situation from all angles over the course of a week, trying to resolve the issue.

One student was especially impressed by a letter in the editorial section. A disabled person had praised her own parents for their efforts on her behalf. The student used the letter as a framework for a journal response that allowed him to finally understand where he stood on the issue and bring closure to an intensely personal and emotional journey. The vivid metaphors signal the clarity of his perception, the struggle to see through the eyes of another, and the power of personal response.

Response to a newspaper letter to the editor, Nov. 19

I have the most respect for the girl writing this letter for the careful and thorough explaining of what life means to people who are disabled.

People who are disabled have a life of their own. They lead a different life than others but they should have the same rights as any other human being.

Trying to imagine how it would feel to be disabled is like trying to imagine a color you've never seen before.

I guess life can be unfair to a lot of people. If you believe in a god and can communicate with your god, tell god he's unfair and cruel.

In my opinion, being disabled would be more painful than being non-existent. Being disabled would be like a program on a computer that is missing certain files. It does not work the same.

Student Guideline

Responding to Newspapers

Read through the newspaper you've chosen. When you're finished, think about how you went about reading the paper, what you read and what you didn't, and how you were attracted or repelled by what you found. As you frame your responses, you may find some of the following questions helpful.

- When did you feel impatient, amused, frustrated, irritated, angry, disbelieving, or moved, and why did you feel that way?

- What sections did you read and which ones did you skip over?

- What ads, types of stories, photos, headlines, or other features grabbed your attention?

- What did you actually find compared with what you expected to find?

- What interests/attitudes/feelings seemed to surface regularly as you flipped through the paper?

- What sections/articles/ads seemed to be written with you or someone like you in mind? Which ones seemed to be meant for a different audience? How could you tell?

- How was the material highlighted or presented to appeal to a particular group or to highlight a particular point of view?

- Was anything unfair in what you read? If there was, why did you feel that way about it?

Some people like to say, "It's not the cards you're dealt but how you play them." But how are these children supposed to play their cards? The way I see things, they weren't even dealt any cards.

I don't agree with the killing of children by their parents. The girl's letter makes me think that it is right to at least give them a chance to live a life with limited skills and a chance for some sort of life. I bow my head to the girl's parents for their efforts.

Kwo Fung (age 12)

Response journals let students make connections

While students might see a play, read a newspaper, and watch some television one day and, the next day, read part of a book, flip through a magazine, and see a movie, none of these events occurs in isolation. Each meaning-filled event is connected to every other event and to all the other incidents, encounters, and discoveries that each day brings each one of us. Just as the ripples from hundreds of pebbles dropped simultaneously into a pond will crisscross and intersect in multiple combinations and permutations, the implications and adjustments that flow from every learning experience will interact with every other learning experience in ways we can't predict or imagine.

Response journals encourage the cross-fertilization and serendipitous intersection of experiences. The more opportunities students have to record, reflect on, and respond to a wide variety of experiences, the more skillful they become at mining these activities for the added insights and understanding that enable them to grow and mature. While the directed activities in this chapter may have stimulated in students some self-awareness, a recognition of the power of mass and live media, and, in some cases, a healthy skepticism about their media influences, the test of their effectiveness will be the extent to which students discover empowerment through the personal response process. Through response journals, students can continue to explore the social and cultural "ripples" they encounter each day and attempt to assess their impact and their value.

5

Developing discussion skills through response journals

Many teachers introduce response journals in the context of their reading programs. As the technique takes hold, however, they inevitably discover that the format is easily and effectively applied to all aspects of their language arts/English programs.

Response journals work well in cooperative learning, a viable strategy in language arts. Whenever and however students are attempting to clarify, discover, assess, reflect on, resolve, and refine what they really think and feel about experience, as they do when learning cooperatively, response journals have a role to play in the process.

Cooperative learning is the umbrella term for students collaborating through talk. Through small-group activities, students interact with and learn from one another, in the process creating a powerful, problem-solving, group dynamic. By collaborating on a regular basis in pairs and in groups of up to five or six, students can develop the interactive skills necessary to share and build on the foundation of each other's interests, backgrounds, experiences, and insights.

Cooperative learning, effective with all age groups, has consistently produced these benefits:

- improved learning results, especially for average students and students "at risk"
- higher academic achievement
- more effective problem solving
- increased higher-level thinking skills
- more positive attitudes toward subjects
- greater motivation to learn

Response journals can help the small-group discussions that characterize cooperative learning in classes across the curriculum in three ways: (1) They can be used to focus on the dynamics of a group, regardless of the content of the discussion or task; (2) in certain circumstances, they can allow an individual to comment on the course of the group's investigations; and (3) they provide a forum for individuals to add further observations, analysis, or comments at the conclusion of a group's deliberations.

Journals help focus on group dynamics

Response journals help develop successful small-group discussions. These discussions don't just happen; they develop as a result of careful planning, positive coaching, and lots of practice. Reflection is an important component.

Discussions are an effective way to foster learning. During discussions, ideas are examined, analyzed, reformulated, and defined in individual, personal, and essential ways. To fully understand concepts, students need to toss out and test ideas or think aloud in their own form of informal discourse. Both formal and informal conferences contribute to the learning.

Whatever the format, students need frequent opportunities to discuss with someone else what they're reading, viewing, writing, listening to, observing, representing, thinking, or doing. Some of the ways in which these interactions might take place are outlined below:

- in pairs, small groups, combined groups, and, when appropriate, in large groups
- in teacher-student conferences, requested either by teacher or student
- in student-student conferences, as students learn to value and seek out peer opinion and advice

Participants in each small group can be selected by the teacher, randomly, or by the participants themselves.

When teachers choose who works with whom, they usually do so for two reasons. Sometimes, they are attempting to redress some kind of perceived imbalance, such as exclusionary same-gender partnerships or constant equivalent-ability groupings. At other times, they are trying to correct potentially counterproductive situations, such as long-standing friendships interfering with group process or ESL students needing the stimulation of first-language users.

Hard and fast rules, however, should be avoided. For some students, initially working with a friend or someone of similar ability may inject a needed sense of security and trust and encourage risk taking. On the other hand, some teachers worry about placing students of differing ability together, concerned that the more highly functioning student gains little from the partnership. The opposite is actually the case: in any mentoring situation, the mentor benefits most.

Clearly, teachers need to make their decisions about groupings based on their students' individual needs, abilities, and personalities. Some teachers begin the year by selecting all groupings themselves and, as individuals learn more about each other and grow comfortable in a variety of groupings, gradually introduce student self-selection. Other teachers begin with random groups or student self-selection and intercede only as circumstances warrant.

Whatever their approach, teachers should ensure that students experience a variety of group partners and that they receive instruction in how to operate responsibly and effectively in such small-group, discussion situations.

Writing responses should reinforce, not replace discussion

Special care is advised when using a written component to a small-group discussion. If students believe that a group discussion is simply a precursor to a written assignment, they will immediately focus on the written assignment and complete the discussion activity in a cursory and perfunctory manner. The value of the discussion is lost.

If there is a written component based on the content of a discussion, be sure you've articulated for yourself and for your students the purpose of that component. Ensure that the status of the discussion remains inviolate.

Before examining in more detail the role of response journals in developing small-group discussion skills, consider some of the taboos and desirable practices of recording the content of discussions about literature.

What not to do

- *Don't* ask students to transcribe the course of the discussion. That kind of activity is usually assigned as a test of how well students were following and contributing to the discussion. As well as undercutting and devaluing the process of the discussion, this approach forces students into needless duplication. Eventually, the attitude in the group becomes "the less we say, the less we'll have to write."
- *Don't* treat discussions as rehearsals for essay writing. A discussion is a complete learning/teaching experience in itself. If you plan to have students write an essay after a discussion, the purpose for that discussion becomes preparation for writing. Obviously, there's nothing wrong with brainstorming, webbing, and other prewriting activities. Just don't confuse them with personal response.
- *Don't* ask students to "report" on other students in their response journals, either in terms of what they say or how they behave in discussion groups. Cooperative learning operates on a basis of trust and respect. If a group is operating inefficiently, other techniques can be used to turn the experience into a positive learning opportunity.

What to do

- *Do* ask students to record the date and topic of each discussion and the names of the members of their groups each time. This basic tracking function keeps the journal record complete and can be performed before or after a discussion.
- *Do* give students an opportunity, if they choose, to record information after a discussion for later use. They may want to record such items as titles of books, surprising or intriguing facts, a reminder to look up a disputed fact, or a sudden thought or memory stimulated by the discussion.
- *Do* encourage students to trade, read, and, with the permission of the owner, extend a small-group discussion into a "paired" dialogue by corresponding in their journals.
- *Do* use the response journal to help students develop effective small-group discussion skills.

What are small-group discussion skills?

In *Learning to Work in Groups*, Matthew Miles identifies five functions that groups perform and which each group member, at various times, needs to supply. When group members accept the responsibility for fulfilling these functions as needed, the group operates efficiently.

Students need to be aware of the different roles they have to play in a group and to be given opportunities to play them. The key small-group discussion roles are *sharing with others, replying to others, leading others, supporting others,* and *evaluating the group's progress.*

Introduce students to each of these roles one by one and give them an opportunity to practise one set of skills before focusing on another. Posting the skills in the classroom is an effective way of demonstrating how valued they are in the environment. Students should also have their own copy for reference. They will then know just what they need to focus on in order to be effective and responsible members of a small-group discussion. See "How to Develop Small-Group Discussion Skills," next page.

How do response journals further small-group discussion skills?

Response journals play an important role in developing small-group discussion skills. Prior to a discussion, you might highlight one of the categories, for example, sharing with others.

During discussions I will **share** with others in my group by . . .

- freely offering my opinions, feelings, or special knowledge;
- listening carefully so I can link up what I know to what they know;
- giving facts and reasons to support my opinions.

After the discussion, ask students to record in their response journals such items as whether or not they practised those skills, how well they succeeded or why they didn't, and what they would try to do in future to improve their performance in that particular response role. Remember that students should comment only on their own performance, not on that of a peer's.

You can compare each student's observations with your own perceptions and discuss them with the student during individual conferences. Over time, the response journal entries will present you with a profile of each student's involvement in group discussions, the degree to which a student is developing self-awareness, the personal goals a student sets, and the kind of success a student is finding in this area.

The guideline "Responding to Small-Group Discussions," on page 76, introduces students to the routines involved in responding to a small-group discussion.

With younger students, such guidelines should be tailored for their stage of readiness or eliminated. Having a discussion about everyone sharing in the talking during small-group work, for example, is enough to focus students on one important aspect of group process.

Developing, refining, and maintaining efficient and effective group skills is a complex process that evolves over a lifetime. Each step in the process, however small, is important.

Student Guideline

How to Develop Small-Group Discussion Skills

During discussions I will **share** with others in my group by . . .

- freely offering my opinions, feelings, or special knowledge;
- listening carefully so I can link up what I know to what they know;
- giving facts and reasons to support my opinions.

During discussions I will **reply** effectively to others in my group by . . .

- listening carefully so that I can ask clarifying questions or make clarifying statements;
- responding freely to other people's questions, interests, problems, and concerns;
- sharing equally in the talking.

During discussions I will show **leadership** in my group by . . .

- suggesting my own ideas, other ways to solve problems, or new directions for the group to explore;
- speaking up without cutting someone off or interfering with the progress the group is making;
- offering suggestions without dominating the discussion.

During discussions I will **support** others in my group by . . .

- helping another person have his or her turn to speak;
- speaking up without cutting off another person or too abruptly changing the subject;
- indicating in my gestures, facial expressions, or my posture that I'm interested in what is being said;
- giving people credit when they deserve it, even if they disagree with me.

During discussions I will **evaluate** my group's progress by . . .

- indicating whether or not I agree with ideas and decisions and my reasons for taking that position;
- considering how well the group is working and how I might help the group work even more effectively;
- re-examining my own opinions and decisions and adjusting them when someone comes up with better ideas.

Student Guideline

Responding to Small-Group Discussions

- Before each small-group discussion, please record in your journal the date, the topic under discussion, and the names of the members of your group.

- Before the discussion, please choose a particular skill you plan to practise. Choose one skill only for each discussion and begin with the skills requiring the most practice. After the discussion, indicate in your journal how well you succeeded in practising that skill, review your own performance in the discussion, and note what you might try to improve on next time.

- After a discussion, you may want to record a piece of information, such as a book title, a sudden thought or memory, a surprising or intriguing fact, or a further comment you weren't able to make during the discussion.

- Please do *not* comment on the performance of another group member.

In the response below, a young student reveals how tentative she feels in groups. Merely acknowledging that she feels as uncomfortable not speaking up in groups as she does speaking up is an important step in her developing self-awareness. For the teacher, this response would be a signal to begin emphasizing support skills with the class. The way this thrust translates in a group is that everyone has the responsibility to encourage others to speak, to indicate interest in what they have to say, and to credit others' contributions, even when disagreement arises. An emphasis on support helps build a sense of collaboration and trust.

Response to a small-group discussion

I get kind of scared in groups because I don't want to be wrong when I say things and people could call me stupid. I talk a lot with my best friend and my second-best friend because your friends don't care if you're shy sometimes and your friends keep your secrets. But my best friend last year did tell a secret and I really felt terrible and we're not best friends anymore so you don't always know. I don't think there's anything wrong with being shy in groups, but I think people sometimes think I don't know things because I just sit there and smile. Groups are really hard.

Jasmin (age 9)

The following response to a small-group discussion shows that the student has been thinking about her role in the group. The student notes what aspect of group process she was trying to focus on and evaluates her performance.

Her response clearly illustrates the value of helping students reflect on their own learning processes. By focusing on how she learns, Tiffany can affect how *well* she learns. Her self-analysis is both thoughtful and sincere, particularly perceptive for an eleven-year-old. Notice, as well, that progress occurs as a process over time.

Response to a small-group discussion
Group members: Barb, Jack, Rahim, Karen
Topic: The poem "Flight One"
Date: Sept. 30

I felt more comfortable with the group today. I still have a hard time butting in when someone's talking but I don't know what else to do when we ramble on and on. I think the first thing I have to do is stop talking when I've said what I want to say. I was really trying to listen to other people today and to add things on to what they said. They really appreciated that because it wasn't all you talk, I talk, you talk, I talk. It was more like it was all mixed up and part of the same argument.

The idea of sharing went well too. When a disagreement occurred it wasn't I'm right and you're wrong. We seemed to be able to say that it's not necessary for everyone to agree or think the same. I guess it helps when there's no right answer. I mentioned yesterday that I have this habit of only talking to one person in a group and that I kept repeating ideas when I didn't know what else to say. I thought it went better today. We had a good discussion.

Tiffany (age 11)

Private reflections promote better group experiences

The first and most difficult concept for students to learn about working effectively in small groups is that saying what they think about an issue is only the beginning. All students have important thoughts, feelings, and opinions they want to share. Naturally enough, they are often far more interested in what they have to say than in what others choose to reply. When they do learn about the full range of group skills and behaviors expected of them, students have to do some serious self-examination and analysis to determine how they function in groups now, how they should be functioning, and what they need to do to close the gap between the two. All of this learning takes time and reflection.

Each group experience has its own challenges, accomplishments, and frustrations that become clearly and fully apparent only when described and acknowledged in a journal entry. Responding in journals about how they performed in groups forces students to become objective about what they're doing and systematic about the steps they need to take to improve. Group problem-solving also often runs counter to an individual's personality and current level of trust in others. Interacting in a group involves much risk taking, revealing more of our thoughts and feelings than we might wish and opening us up to some measure of embarrassment, disapproval, or even rejection. Journals offer students a secure space to express and explore how they feel about group experiences, why they feel that way, and how their feelings might have an impact on their future group interactions.

For many students, the path to success in the public forum of small-group discussions lies in the private deliberations and ruminations of their response journals.

6

Evaluating response journals

Any evaluation system that hopes to facilitate and stimulate the learning process will mirror its complexity.

A comprehensive evaluation system contains a number of interdependent facets. In general, such an evaluation system should encompass the following:

- derive from, reflect, and stimulate specific learning behaviors
- assess both process and product
- address both affective and cognitive behaviors
- match method of evaluation with the nature of the learning objective; e.g., a performance objective should be evaluated through performance
- contain both formative and summative components
- include self- and peer-evaluation elements in formative evaluation
- include self-evaluation as a component of summative evaluation when students have developed the requisite experience and skills
- acknowledge self-evaluation as the eventual goal of all evaluation
- be flexible enough to accommodate the needs of the individual learner
- inform students beforehand how, when, and for what purposes they will be evaluated
- monitor program effectiveness

The usual evaluative methods include observation (anecdotal records, checklists, tracking sheets), questionnaires, results from reading conferences, reading portfolios, and teacher-designed instruments for specific learning objectives.

A wide variety of techniques can be employed when evaluating personal responses by themselves or as proof of progress over time. No evaluative technique, however, is completely objective. Underlying each technique are certain presumptions about learning and a set of specific criteria. Assessment of a reading portfolio, for which a response journal could be used, for example, is subject to a range of interpretation, depending on the criteria being applied and how each is weighted. As teachers employ these techniques, they first need to decide what constitutes evidence of growth in each.

Students need to know how they will be evaluated

Although the intent of formative and summative evaluation is different, summative evaluation can have an important formative outcome. The key lies in defining and declaring clear learning objectives. If students know precisely the criteria by which they will be evaluated, they will more readily direct their efforts to meeting those criteria. If students have the opportunity to *set* some of those criteria themselves, they can assume ownership for the direction of their own learning.

The differences between the two types of evaluation become clear in the following descriptive lists:

Formative Evaluation	Summative Evaluation
• focused on daily, ongoing assessment of student progress	• utilizes records for report card purposes
• focused on daily, ongoing assessment of program effectiveness	• uses comparative standards and judgments
• incorporates a diagnostic function for both student and program	• intended for overall decision-making, e.g., student placement in a specific program or grade
• geared to individual needs and growth	• includes teacher acting as teacher/evaluator
• intended to assist students in learning	
• intended to improve educational experience	
• includes teacher acting as trusted adult partner	

The purpose of formative evaluation is growth in learning. Of all the skills cultivated in schools, however, formative self-evaluation, in which students take over responsibility, to some measure, for their learning, is the most difficult. Objective self-evaluation can only develop over time and with considerable practice.

For students to assume an active role in the learning process, they need to see evaluation as a tool and to feel that they have control over its use. They need to understand how evaluation can help them and to practise self-evaluation on a regular basis.

Formative self-evaluation allows students to gain an objective view of their own performance and to assume some responsibility for the course of their own learning. As they gain in confidence and skill, more mature students will often be able to apply their own criteria in their own way for their own purposes.

For summative evaluation to have a formative function, the evaluation system must be transparent. Right from the start, students should know not only what response journals are and why and how they will be used, but, most importantly, how they will be evaluated. Their own suggestions for implementing and operating the journals should also be considered. If possible, the group or individuals might suggest or select some of the evaluation criteria.

Whatever teachers want to happen in journals should be clearly articulated and those criteria built into the evaluation system. If objectives are clearly stated, evaluation can direct and support the learning process. For example, if students should be reviewing past entries and reflecting on their own growth or changes in their opinions, they should be told in advance to include this kind of item in their journals. They also should be shown the marking scheme and told when their work will be formally evaluated.

During a designated period of perhaps two or three weeks, you could check informally or with self-evaluation checklists, to see if students are including the desired kind of entry in their journals. You could then discuss their progress with them.

After that period, it's time to assign a summative mark for the extent to which each student has met a certain criterion. By discussing with a student how the mark was arrived at and what the student would have to do to improve the mark over the next evaluation period, you could imbue the summative mark with a practical formative function.

Variations in marking emphasis are essential. The evaluation system must be flexible enough to adapt to student needs and growth and continuing program effectiveness. If teachers want to emphasize one specific criterion, for instance, they simply weight it with more marks. As students become more adept at certain kinds of entries, teachers may want to stimulate other uses by changing the mark emphasis.

In collaboration with students before each evaluation period, you could decide which criteria to retain and which to discard. You could even individualize the marking scheme for particular students to stimulate a specific aspect of growth.

Students can help each other meet criteria. They may read designated sections of each other's response journals and discuss how well the criteria are being met. They may even offer suggestions for improvement.

One of the most important features of response journals is that they supply concrete evidence of a process over time. To stimulate process objectives, be sure to include process as well as product criteria in your evaluation scheme.

What are the best ways to process journal entries?

Once the routines of using response journals have been established and students are reading and responding regularly, teachers have to decide how best to process the entries that students are producing.

Collecting a set of journals every three or four weeks has several drawbacks. With up to a dozen entries for each journal, the time and effort required to read through a class set is preclusive, and that's without even dealing with the issue of marking. Besides, with that length of time between markings, students have little chance of benefitting from formative evaluation and improving their performance.

Most teachers find that if they read five or six journals every second day or a couple each day, they're able to stay current. In some cases, a simple comment or question on a Post-it note can be integrated into the routine. Student/teacher conferences, of course, offer another opportunity to discuss relevant issues arising from the teacher's review of journal entries.

Marking the content of the journals daily is problematic. Teachers want to let students know at what level they're functioning in their journals and what they need to do to improve. To maintain the formative intent of such marking, however, teachers should refrain from making summative judgments or assigning specific grades. That should be reserved for gathering data for reporting periods.

Teachers need to keep marking fast and efficient to stay on top of the quantity of material. Devising and posting a simple rubric divided into levels and explained with criteria and a percentage range for each level is a popular solution. The levels are linked to the performance criteria already established and introduced. A check mark or color code will indicate to students how well they're progressing. The rubric contains the information necessary for students to understand what they need to do to improve.

The sample rubric on the next page names the levels for clarification and includes a possible mark range. In actual classroom use, each level might be a different color or a series of check marks from one to four. Since a letter designature, such as A, B, C, or D, carries many summative connotations and denotations, it should be avoided.

The sample arbitrarily employs four levels. Students at any one level will often display characteristics from another level. The degree to which their profiles overlap determines whether or not they would be achieving at the lower or upper end of the mark range. Teachers should match their own levels with their corresponding summative reporting standards.

Once students have become familiar with responding routines and have received sufficient input from the teacher, they are ready to engage in some formative self-evaluation.

At regular intervals, ask your students to step back and evaluate their own responses on the basis of the outlined objectives. They can review their own progress, assess the extent to which they are meeting the objectives, and set new goals for themselves. At different times, you can have them isolate and examine one aspect of their journals or take an overall look at all aspects.

The series of instruments beginning on page 84 demonstrates a few methods for initiating this kind of self-examination. The first instrument (page 84) serves as an introduction to self-evaluation. The second (page 85) uses selected criteria and a few cueing questions to assist students in a more defined self-evaluation process. The third, more comprehensive instrument (page 86) allows older students to focus on the specifics of their responding patterns and gather the information necessary to set some practical goals.

For consistency and reinforcement, the same instrument can then be adapted, as the fourth instrument, on page 87, illustrates, to serve in the teacher's summative evaluation of a student's responses.

The final instrument in this series (page 88) demonstrates how summative criteria can be selected and weighted to emphasize participation in specific features of the program during a particular period.

Teacher Guideline

Sample Daily Marking Rubric

Level	Percentage Range	Criteria
Non-compliant	below 50%	– insufficient reading – insufficient number and/or length of responses – content of responses perfunctory and superficial – student/teacher conference required
Compliant	50–65%	– sufficient reading accomplished – tracking functions complete – sufficient number and length of responses – responses characterized by frequent retelling, likes and dislikes, occasional relating to personal experience, some prediction
Extended	66–79%	– all compliance routines established plus some additional reading and responding – responses additionally characterized by brief retelling when necessary, frequent relating to personal experience, prediction, and offering reasons for opinions and conclusions
Independent	80% +	– all compliance routines established – all extended routines established plus considerable additional reading and responding – responses additionally characterized by recognition of characters' motivations, image and description patterns, linking of cause and effect, opinions often supported by evidence from the text, awareness of author's purposes apparent

Student Checklist

The Right Track for Reading

Evaluation from _____ to _____

1. How much have you read over this period?

2. What kind(s) of book(s) have you been reading?

3. How do you feel about the amount and type of reading you've been doing? (Please check one box and comment on why you feel that way.)

   ❑ Satisfied   ❑ Somewhat Satisfied   ❑ Dissatisfied

4. How do you feel about the kinds of responses you've been making to your reading? (Again, check one box and comment on why you feel that way.)

   ❑ Satisfied   ❑ Somewhat Satisfied   ❑ Dissatisfied

5. What goal(s) do you think you should set for your future reading and responding?

Student Checklist

Evaluating Reading Responses Further

Evaluation from _____ to _____

Please circle the choice that best describes your responses for this period.

When I'm responding to my own reading or to readalouds, how often do I . . .

	Never	Sometimes	Often	Quite Often
• write extended responses (1/2 page or more)?	1	2	3	4
• retell the plot?	1	2	3	4
• relate my own real-life, related experiences?	1	2	3	4
• explain how my own experiences added to my understanding?	1	2	3	4
• predict what might happen next?	1	2	3	4
• comment on why characters act the way they do?	1	2	3	4
• support my opinions with evidence from the story (e.g., incidents, images, character's actions or decisions)?	1	2	3	4

After completing this checklist, record in your journal what you noticed about the kinds of responses you normally make and the kinds of responses you should attempt more often. Comment, as well, on the number and length of your responses and the amount of reading you're doing.

Student Checklist

Taking a Hard Look at Reading Responses

Evaluation from _____ to _____

Please circle the choice that best describes your responses for this period.

When I'm responding to my own reading or to readalouds, how often do I . . .

	Never	Sometimes	Often	Quite Often
• write extended responses (1/2 page or more)?	1	2	3	4
• retell the plot?	1	2	3	4
• relate my own real-life, related experiences?	1	2	3	4
• explain how my own experiences added to my understanding?	1	2	3	4
• predict what might happen next?	1	2	3	4
• give reasons for my predictions?	1	2	3	4
• link *what* happens with *why* it happens?	1	2	3	4
• separate fact from opinion?	1	2	3	4
• comment on why characters act the way they do?	1	2	3	4
• recognize patterns of behavior?	1	2	3	4
• identify recurring images or descriptions?	1	2	3	4
• talk about what the author's purposes might be?	1	2	3	4
• support my opinions with evidence from the story (e.g., incidents, images, character's actions or decisions)	1	2	3	4

Teacher Checklist

Summative Evaluation of Reading Responses 1

Student Name: _____

Please circle the choice that best describes this student's responses for the period

from _____ to _____

When responding to reading or to readalouds, how effectively does this student . . .

	Not Very	To Some Extent	Reasonably	Effectively	Very Effectively
• write extended responses (1/2 page or more)?	1	2	3	4	5
• retell the plot?	1	2	3	4	5
• relate own real-life, related experiences?	1	2	3	4	5
• explain how own experiences added to understanding?	1	2	3	4	5
• predict what might happen next?	1	2	3	4	5
• give reasons for predictions?	1	2	3	4	5
• link *what* happens *with* why it happens?	1	2	3	4	5
• separate fact from opinion?	1	2	3	4	5
• comment on why characters act the way they do?	1	2	3	4	5
• recognize patterns of behavior?	1	2	3	4	5
• identify recurring images or descriptions?	1	2	3	4	5
• talk about what the author's purposes might be?	1	2	3	4	5
• support opinions with evidence from the story? (e.g., incidents, images, character's actions or decisions)	1	2	3	4	5

Teacher Checklist

Summative Evaluation of Reading Responses 2

Student Name: _____

Evaluation from _____ to _____

To what extent has the student . . .

- responded to a sufficient number of activities (at least three extended responses per cycle) ?

| 10 | 8 | 6 | 4 | 2 | 0 |

- read a sufficient amount?

| 30 | 25 | 20 | 15 | 10 | 0 |

- responded to independent reading and readalouds in a detailed, varied, and thoughtful manner?

| 20 | 17 | 14 | 11 | 8 | 0 |

- made insightful connections, used responses to think through issues, demonstrated in-depth understanding?

| 15 | 12 | 9 | 6 | 3 | 0 |

Total   /75

Students improve their reading, first and foremost, by reading.

A reading inventory such as that shown on page 19 allows teachers to monitor what and how much students are reading. The student guideline "How to Use Response Journals" instructed students to keep a running inventory in the back of their journals of the reading they completed. Pertinent information should have been added as they finished material.

Possibly each month, students can review their reading patterns by reflecting on their inventories. The next two response guidelines, "Responding to Your Reading Inventory" and "Responding to Your Reading," direct students in formative, self-evaluation exercises based on their reading patterns.

Let students help devise evaluation criteria

If you want your students to "buy into" your program as quickly and as completely as possible, include them in the process of devising evaluation criteria for marks. You can even individualize the criteria.

How much you do in this regard or when you start will depend on your individual class, their age, and their stage of readiness. The process unfolds simply.

1. Brainstorm a list of criteria with your students. Through discussion, prioritize and short-list the items.
2. To individualize the marking scheme, reserve a certain amount (perhaps 25 percent) for items not chosen by you.
3. Ask each student to add items worth that amount to an individual marking scheme.

The marks sheet on page 92 illustrates how the teacher and student can each select criteria to be used in the teacher's evaluation for summative purposes.

Student Formative Self-evaluation Guideline

Responding to Your Reading Inventory

Please look over your reading inventory. Total the number of books and the number of pages you've read. Write a response in your journal discussing what you notice about your reading. The answers to the following questions should form part of your response:

- How much have you read compared to what you thought you had read? How does the amount you're reading compare with how much you are expected to read? Do you need to adjust how much you're reading? How?

- What kinds of books do you normally read? Why do you usually read these kinds of books? Are there certain types you don't read at all? Have your reading tastes changed since last year? If so, how?

- What titles do you remember with particular pleasure? Why?

- How could you broaden your reading tastes? What kinds of books could you choose?

- After reviewing your reading inventory, what specific reading goals should you set for yourself for the next month? What plan can you establish to reach your goals?

Student Formative Self-evaluation Guideline

Responding to Your Reading

Evaluation from _____ to _____

1. How much have you read over this period? (How many pages)

2. What kinds of material have you been reading? (Please check.)

   ❏ Novels   ❏ Anthologies   ❏ Magazines   ❏ Non-fiction

   ❏ Other (Please list.)

3. How do you feel about the amount and type of reading you've been doing? (Please check one box and comment on why you feel that way.)

   ❏ Satisfied   ❏ Somewhat Satisfied   ❏ Dissatisfied

4. How do you feel about the number and quality of the responses you've been making to your reading? (Please check one box and comment on why you feel that way.)

   ❏ Satisfied   ❏ Somewhat Satisfied   ❏ Dissatisfied

5. After reviewing your reading and responding, what specific goals do you think you need to set for your efforts over the next few weeks?

Summative Evaluation Based on Shared Criteria

Independent Reading Marks Sheet

Student Name: _____

Evaluation from _____ to _____

Teacher-chosen criteria

To what extent do your entries indicate that you have . . .

- kept a complete record of the titles of each independent reading selection
  and the amount read?   /5

- included a number of personal responses to independent reading selections
  (at least three per week)?   /5

- read a sufficient amount?   /15

- responded to reading in a varied, thoughtful, and insightful manner?   /15

Student-chosen criteria

To what extent do my entries indicate that I have . . .

- *read a lot of different kinds of material for independent reading?*   /5
- *read to younger students as part of a buddy-reading project?*   /5

                                                                    Total: /50

Evaluation should encompass journal extensions

As noted earlier, for response journals to play a key role in the development of such areas as small-group discussion skills and media literacy, the evaluation system must reflect that involvement.

Listening and speaking are the most difficult language arts components to evaluate, however. Whether for formative or summative purposes, the key to evaluation in the areas of discussion and media lies in identifying the discrete skills and behaviors that the students need to master. Once identified, these behaviors can be monitored and practised, and their growth measured.

Formative self-evaluation develops gradually over time and only after considerable practice. Teachers should consciously promote as many opportunities as possible for their students to do self-evaluation.

In the first checklist that follows, students are invited to consider the depth of their responses to media. In the next two instruments, they are asked to reflect on how well they are applying a specific set of skills in their small-group discussions. They could then review their own progress, assess the extent to which they are meeting the objectives, and set new goals for themselves. Both these instruments rely on familiarity with the small-group discussion skills outlined in Chapter 5. The first relatively simple instrument requires the student to identify and apply a variety of skills. In the second instrument, three discrete skills are comprehensively reviewed. Teachers can substitute any of the skills from Chapter 5 as the need arises.

Student Checklist

Formative Evaluation of Media Responses

Evaluation from _____ to _____

To what extent do your media responses indicate how well you are able to . . .

	Extremely Well			Not Very Well	
• relate media events to personal experience	5	4	3	2	1
• recognize the central meaning of or purpose behind events	5	4	3	2	1
• recall and explain the importance of significant details	5	4	3	2	1
• recognize bias	5	4	3	2	1
• identify cause-and-effect relationships	5	4	3	2	1
• distinguish fact from opinion	5	4	3	2	1
• compare and contrast elements of different media events	5	4	3	2	1

Student Guideline

Evaluating My Small-Group Discussion Skills

Date of discussion:

Topic of discussion:

Group participants:

Three skills I applied well

Three skills I hope to improve

-
-
-

Student Guideline

Evaluating Your Performance in Small-Group Discussions

Please consider your usual performance in a small-group discussion and circle your choice.

A. How often do you . . .   (Always, Often, Sometimes, Not Often, Never)

- go out of your way to help another person have his or her turn to speak?   A   O   S   N/O   N

- speak up without cutting off another person or too abruptly changing the subject?   A   O   S   N/O   N

- indicate in your gestures, facial expressions, or posture that you're interested in what is being said?   A   O   S   N/O   N

- give people credit when they deserve it, even if they disagree with you?   A   O   S   N/O   N

B. How difficult is it for you to . . .   (Extremely, Very, Somewhat, Difficult at Times, Not Difficult at All)

- go out of your way to help another person have his or her turn to speak?   E   V   S   D/T   N/D

- speak up without cutting off another person or too abruptly changing the subject?   E   V   S   D/T   N/D

- indicate in your gestures, facial expressions, or posture that you're interested in what is being said?   E   V   S   D/T   N/D

- give people credit when they deserve it, even if they disagree with you?   E   V   S   D/T   N/D

C. How successfully do you . . .   (Extremely, Very, Somewhat, Successfully at Times, Not Successful at All)

- go out of your way to help another person have his or her turn to speak?   E   V   S   S/T   N/S

- speak up without cutting off another person or too abruptly changing the subject?   E   V   S   S/T   N/S

- indicate in your gestures, facial expressions, or posture that you're interested in what is being said?   E   V   S   S/T   N/S

- give people credit when they deserve it, even if they disagree with you?   E   V   S   S/T   N/S

The following criteria for summative evaluation reflect the wide potential of response journals. The list, however, is not meant to be exhaustive. The criteria you choose will reflect the particular program objectives in place during a specific period.

Sample Summative Evaluation Criteria

To what extent do the entries indicate that the student has

- kept a complete record of the titles of each independent reading selection and the amount read each period?
- included a variety of responses to reading selections?
- kept a complete record of media experiences (e.g., film, television, or video viewing)?
- kept track of her/his role in group discussion, reviewed past performances, and attempted to strengthen specific skills?
- recorded questions/comments/observations for later reference (e.g., for student/teacher conferences)?
- looked back at previous entries and attempted to reflect on those experiences/opinions/emotions?

By selecting a variety of criteria, teachers can develop formative and summative instruments that value and reward a range of journal components.

The next two instruments demonstrate how to evaluate the full range of response journal entries.

The intent of the first instrument is formative. When several criteria are involved, students need help in identifying all the components and assessing their ongoing work with each. The formative evaluation lets them determine how well they're doing at present and where they need to focus their future efforts.

The intent of the second instrument is summative. Teachers can use it to sum up how well students have been handling each criterion. The evaluative cycle is complete, of course, when students employ the marks from each discrete item to guide where and how they need to improve.

Student Formative Self-evaluation Guideline

Overall Assessment of Response Journal Work

Evaluation from _____ to _____

For each of the following questions, please circle the appropriate mark.
To what extent do your entries indicate that you have . . .

- read a sufficient amount?

    10   8   6   4   2   0

- responded to independent reading and readalouds in a detailed, varied, and thoughtful manner?

    10   8   6   4   2   0

- made insightful connections, used responses to think through issues, and demonstrated in-depth understanding

    related to independent reading?   10   8   6   4   2   0

    related to media events?   10   8   6   4   2   0

- described your performance in small groups objectively and thoroughly?

    10   8   6   4   2   0

- reviewed past discussions and attempted to improve your skills?

    10   8   6   4   2   0

For what area(s) should you set new goals?

How do you plan to meet the objectives in these areas more completely?

Summative Evaluation Based on Stated Criteria for All Aspects of Response Journals

Student Name: _____

Evaluation from _____ to _____

1. Independent (individual) Reading
- keeps daily records

Complete					Incomplete
5	4	3	2	1	0

- reads sufficient amount

Beyond Requirements					Insufficient
5	4	3	2	1	0

- varies responses

Often					Never
5	4	3	2	1	0

- responds thoughtfully and insightfully

Often					Never
10	8	6	4	2	0

2. Readalouds
- responds thoughtfully and insightfully

Often					Never
5	4	3	2	1	0

3. Small-Group Discussions
- describes performance objectively and thoroughly

Often					Never
5	4	3	2	1	0

- reviews past discussions and attempts to improve skills

Often					Never
5	4	3	2	1	0

4. Media
- responds thoughtfully and insightfully

Often					Never
5	4	3	2	1	0

5. In General
- looks back, reflects, and builds on previous entries

Often					Never
5	4	3	2	1	0

Comments: Please use the back of this sheet.

Mark: /50

All evaluation leads to self-evaluation

The goal of all evaluation is the development of self-evaluation. When students are knowledgeable, realistic, and dispassionate about their own progress, the summative evaluation system holds no surprises. Students themselves decide how best to measure their own learning and judge the worth of what they achieve.

In the following journal entry, a student reflects on the summative term evaluation of her response journal. With a limited number of criteria in the previous term, the student had scored perfect in all categories. As the teacher introduced additional journal applications, however, the evaluation criteria grew and the expectations were modified. Since the student realized how the expectations had changed and had already identified for herself how personal success should be defined, she still reacted to her new evaluation with understanding and pride.

Response to a journal term evaluation, April 22

I think I did well on this journal evaluation. I got perfect last time because there were only 4 categories to be marked in and each one was worth a lot. This one was different. It had more categories and I didn't score perfect on all of them. I'm proud of my mark anyway. What I think is most important about writing a response is the insight and depth of thought and I do well in that area. I'm glad I can look into a book and dig up details when I read, but I have no idea how I developed that skill. Maybe it's the amount of reading I do. Who knows?

Jessica (age 12)

Mature self-evaluation depends on students having many opportunities to critically examine their own work using the same criteria that the teacher uses for summative evaluation. When response journals are used for a variety of purposes and the scoring rubrics reflect the complexity of the program, students find it even harder to keep track of all the evaluative threads. Teachers can support the growth of self-evaluation by regularly administering teacher-made, self-evaluation instruments, requesting periodic progress appraisals from students in the form of response journal entries, and addressing students' perceptions of their progress in regular, student-teacher conferences. Finally, teachers should respect the fact that students naturally grow into self-evaluation at different rates and to varying degrees. The final ingredients in supporting this growth over years are understanding and patience.

7

Putting response journals into a larger classroom context

Response journals operate most effectively in a flexible, integrated classroom environment. The recursive nature of reading/writing processes does not permit easy pigeonholing. Processing language is also unpredictable. As much as you try to plan and organize the process, language tends to spill over the edges of your timetable and "wrinkle" your routines. When that happens, you need to emphasize the function and let the form adapt.

The function of any classroom activity is simply stated: *to arrive at meaning*. The focal point is the meaning students are deriving from print and talk, the meaning encapsulated in their writing, and the meaning of what they say. The classroom should be a place for processing language. To learn about language, students need to use language; they need to talk and listen and read and write as much as possible. Teaching the mechanics of language is an important component of the process, of course, but it should happen in the context of a student's actual language and never obscure or devalue the primary focus on meaning.

Students need daily opportunities to read, talk, listen to, and write about themes with which they can personally relate. Each student is leading a specific and particular life; if you can make contact with that life and tap it, the language will flow.

What marks an effective classroom environment?

An effective learning/teaching environment moulds itself to student needs. Rich and flexible, it is supportive of and conducive to the complex ways in which students learn. The following characteristics are true of it.

There is time for students to interact with their peers as they learn, ensuring that learning occurs cooperatively in pairs and small groups.

Cooperative learning strategies, which focus on peer collaboration, have been shown to contribute to higher academic achievement, increase self-esteem, improve social skills, and facilitate language development. Teachers who hope to effectively counter bias, discrimination, and bigotry of all kinds in their classroom should make the small-group instructional techniques that characterize cooperative learning a mainstay of their programs.

Students have opportunities to make decisions and solve problems related to the classroom experience.

Students who are constantly reacting to decisions others make for them have difficulty accepting responsibility for whatever goes on in the classroom and school environments. They can learn to take responsibility for their own learning only when they are offered opportunities to assume responsible roles.

If a specific unit or text is received with muted enthusiasm and reluctant involvement, for example, pinpointing the problems and suggesting solutions should involve the students. If they're part of the solution, students will ensure that the solution works. Self- and peer-evaluation, especially formative evaluation, are also essential growth activities.

When students are actively involved in learning as a problem-solving process, moreover, they are more apt to accept responsibility for the interactions that occur in their environment. Racist behavior or homophobic harassment, for example, are not someone else's problems; they affect everyone.

There is a degree of independent choice and responsibility for what, when, and how the individual learns.

Knowing how to make good choices is an essential life skill and one that will develop only when real opportunities to make choices are regularly provided. The classroom program needs to be flexible enough to recognize and match individual needs, interests, and learning styles. In any event, try to build in choice or student input whenever possible, including components such as texts, teaching pace, learning/teaching techniques, and related follow-up activities.

Keep in mind, however, that making good choices is a skill acquired over time. If unfortunate choices are made, they can be turned into learning opportunities. Students accustomed to making choices without risk and on a regular basis make choices that are mature and effective.

Students have time to reflect on what and how they are learning.

As noted earlier, language and learning are intrinsically linked. To fully understand ideas, students need the chance to examine them in their own informal talk or style of writing. Reflection is the soul of the learning process and central to any study of literature. Students need the opportunity and freedom to mull over ideas in a personally significant manner to internalize what they mean and how they relate to their own lives.

The environment is free of gender, racial, cultural, ability, social class, and heterosexual stereotyping.

Students need to feel safe in the classroom environment and valued by their peers and adults.

An insistence on equity helps lay the foundation for a learning/teaching environment in which all share and benefit equally. In this environment, the teacher serves as an example of behavior, displaying, for example, a genuine courtesy toward others and a respect for individual differences.

A basic misunderstanding about teaching is that teachers are able to instruct separately from their personal beliefs and value systems. In reality, the personal and the professional are inextricably intertwined. As a result, teachers need to reflect regularly on their classroom behavior to discover, re-examine, and, if warranted, adjust the way their personal values affect their professional actions.

Students value the learning of others in the classroom and show respect for them.

In any classroom, all students have the right to learn and all students have the right to respect. Students need to feel positive about themselves and their abilities and believe that they are engaged in worthwhile, meaningful, and productive activities.

When teachers discuss the characteristics of a successful learner, they identify attention to models of appropriate learning behavior, positive self-esteem and an ability to "take risks" as crucial elements. The challenge facing teachers is finding ways to support, encourage, nurture, and direct the many, distinct individuals who comprise any classroom.

What makes a viable language classroom program?

If you can answer "yes" to each of the following questions, your program is well balanced, vital, and student-centred. Some of the elements, of course, may be outside your control. With others, however, the checklist might give you an idea or two for fine-tuning your program.

- Does your program include large blocks of time for language arts or English?
- Are there regular opportunities for readalouds, independent, self-selected reading, personal response, writing as process, reading/writing conferences?
- Do you ensure that learning often occurs cooperatively in pairs, small groups, combined groups, and, when appropriate, in a whole-class group?
- Is drama employed whenever possible to facilitate learning?
- Does your program encourage a warm, supportive, accepting atmosphere, free of gender, racial, cultural, ability, class, and heterosexist stereotypes?
- Do you encourage students to make decisions and choices and accept a developing degree of responsibility for what, when, how, and where they learn?
- Do you actively read and write and, then, share with the students how you go about the process?
- Do you have flexible seating/work areas to facilitate cooperative learning?
- Do you take advantage of additional school and community human resources, for example, the teacher-librarian (resource-based learning), authors, and storytellers?

Personal response benefits from a wide range of materials

The breadth of personal response depends upon the availability of materials and equipment. The broader the range and variety of stimulating experiences, the greater the chance that the incredible spectrum of individual differences in any one classroom can be accommodated.

Your students should have access to many different types of print materials at different levels of difficulty and with a variety of themes. They have a right to reading materials that suit their individual abilities, and your program should accommodate a wide range of both reading levels and individual interests. With the following informal checklist, you can review the choices your students have.

novels (many individual titles)	anthologies
newspapers	thesauri
poetry	magazines
picture books	informational books
dictionaries	student-written material
play scripts	

How freely are your students able to access these materials?

Consider, too, whether the following print categories are represented in your program:

- a variety of genres, e.g., mystery, adventure, science fiction, exposition
- books and articles related to the "content" areas, such as history and science
- legends and myths
- fairy tales and folk tales

The availability of audio-visual equipment and resources is desirable too. Can you offer the following?

- audiotapes for listening and recording
- videotapes for viewing and recording
- films, filmstrips, and an overhead projector
- film and video catalogues
- a television set
- television listings
- computers for word processing, research, and e-mail; access to a printer

These open up more ways of accommodating individual differences.

Response journals let students integrate learning

If the same teacher is responsible for teaching in more than one subject area, the organizational problems that can arise due to the division of the school curriculum into separate subject areas can be overcome. From the junior grades on, however, the various "disciplines" are increasingly assigned to different teacher-specialists. Bridging those disciplines and integrating programs then becomes vital to the promotion of effective and efficient learning.

The word *integrated* is used so often in discussing English and language arts programs that the term needs clarification. The term is usually used in three ways.

- An integrated program is a *blend* of all the aspects of English: reading, writing, listening, speaking, viewing, and valuing.
- An integrated program is an *individualized* program related to the personal growth, skills, and cultural needs of the individual student.
- An integrated program is *coordinated* with other aspects of a student's program, such as art, music or science. Conversely, the other aspects of a student's program should be integrated with the English program.

All three aspects of integration stem from the same learning through language concept. The process, representing much more than a "parenthood" concept, is detailed and specific and speaks as much to language programs as it does to learning across the curriculum.

As you reflect on the following basic principles of learning through language, consider how closely they match the principles involved in using response journals.

- To fully understand concepts, students need to "pick away" at ideas or "think aloud" in their own talk or style of writing. Opportunities to talk and write are crucial to real learning.

- Students should feel free to take risks in their writing. They need to express themselves in their own words and feel confident that the meaning of what they say is the focal point of the writing experience.
- During the talking and writing process, ideas are examined, analyzed, reformulated, and defined in very personal, individual, and essential ways.
- A variety of real audiences and a wide range of writing purposes will help students realize the need for writing.
- The use of plain language promotes learning; the jargon of specialized subjects and needlessly technical language tend to inhibit it.

The medium really is the message. With response journals, students can interact with issues and materials regardless of the subject area. The response journal forum is ideal for examining, analyzing, reformulating, and defining in a personal and individual manner.

As the English or language arts teacher, you naturally welcome real problems to solve, opportunities for students to reflect on events, ideas, and values they're confronting every day, and real purposes for talking and writing.

Whatever the subject area, the skills and goals are the same. If overlap occurs, it can only reinforce the learning. Since the English or language arts curriculum can itself become compartmentalized, we need to break down the barriers to real learning wherever they occur.

With this concept of integration in mind, try to capitalize on any opportunities to open the doors of your language classroom not only to the wider world beyond the school walls, but also to the often more isolated worlds of the subject-specialized curriculum.

If you haven't already begun the process, you might want to act on some of the following suggestions.

- Encourage students to comment in their journals on ideas and concepts from other subject areas. Perhaps they could write about questions that arise in history, express a strong opinion they hold on a current issue, or convey impressions of a fictional character or historical figure who appeals to them.
- Suggest that students describe in their journals specific incidents and impressions arising from excursions, drama productions, or other special events. Then encourage them to reread these specific entries and try to encapsulate their impressions, develop a more generalized viewpoint, or offer a revised perspective.
- Encourage students to use their response journals as a sounding board or trial run for writing for a variety of purposes and a wider audience.
- Encourage students to adapt their response journal entries for use in other areas of the writing program, for instance, as a starting point for a personal experience narrative or as the source for a letter.
- Provide opportunities for students who wish to share orally some of their response journal entries with a wider audience. These readings may stimulate lively discussion or result in a vital debate over issues raised.

Response journals can be used to integrate all aspects of the English program. In the next sample, a student decides to discuss the progress of a story she's writing. Her personal ownership of the creative process is evident when she writes about her excitement and satisfaction in producing the exact effects in a reader that she had intended. Equally fascinating is her reason for making this particular entry. She suggests that the act of writing puts her in touch with a concrete, author's perspective she might not otherwise possess.

Response to a writing period
April 17

I have become so ultimately fascinated by a mystery story that I have been writing that I decided to do a little response. As the story progresses, I hope to build suspicion and I think I have succeeded. So far my story really hasn't told too much but I have an idea about a character who is a girl my age who returns to her birthplace where something of the supernatural happened.

Today Mr. L. read my story out loud to me, and to my surprise he interpreted it exactly how I wanted the story to be interpreted. So that really wowed me out. This story is really going to be a shocker, I mean something that you don't expect, something out of the unknown. I hope I succeed. I also want to create a memorable character with a memorable name. When I thought of that, a million names raced through my mind. I just thought that it would be interesting to respond to my story. This way I won't be so anxious for the ending, since I have the author's point of view.

Karen (age 13)

The next entry suggests that a teacher never knows what kind of reading experience will have an impact on a specific student or what that impact might be. The student discovered a book of word puzzles called *Improve Your Lateral Thinking* that shed new light on solving problems. He was especially impressed with one example that also gave him added insight into stereotypes.

Response to reading Improve Your Lateral Thinking
April 17

I think the puzzles in this book are very interesting. They make you think of different solutions. Instead of just answering the question, they make you try to think and look at the problem from different angles.

I especially liked the one about the man and his son. The man and his son went on a plane and the man took his son to visit the pilot. When the man and his son left the cockpit, the pilot said to the co-pilot, "That was my son."

Usually people would think that the pilot was the step-father or that maybe it was a gay couple. But it didn't say anywhere that all pilots had to be male. Everyone just thought it was male because of stereotypes. It turns out the pilot was the boy's mother.

Many of these problems tell you a bit about history and what incidents really occurred. A lot of people would try to think of a very straightforward solution. If a man had to cross a river but he couldn't swim, there wasn't a bridge, and he couldn't use anything around him for a boat or raft, who says the lake couldn't be frozen? Maybe it was frozen and he simply walked across.

Most of the clues are very important. I really would want to read more of these kinds of books and puzzles.

Tommy (age 13)

From where does inspiration spring and what does student ownership of learning mean? The next response answers both questions as well as proving that the insights offered by personal response can happen anywhere and at any time.

Response to an observation
March 7

Let's be honest. I was totally bored. Writing was not my idea of a good time and I didn't know where to start. I checked my rough drafts and list of ideas and nothing turned me on. I just felt lazy and rusty and uninspired. I tried brainstorming. What can you get from a vacuum? I wanted to scream! No, this certainly wasn't my day until Fred came tripping up the aisle and fell flat on his face! It wasn't until he got up, tripped again, and sort of sprawled and stumbled into his seat that the idea came. The way Fred had dramatically fallen reminded me of the time I went skiing and the hilarious time my friends and I had. You wouldn't believe the fall I took and what happened after that! Sometimes I wish I kept a diary. Anyway, thank you, Fred!

Shana (age 13)

In the entry below, notice the value of peer response partners as well as the sense of ownership as the writer makes an important discovery about authors and the perceived originality of their material.

Response to a writing period
November 26

I did something today with a story that I've never done before. Ralph was reading over the latest version of my story, "Dark Spaces." He liked the way things were going until he mentioned that the story sort of jumps in the middle of the action and he couldn't follow what was going on. I looked it over and realized he was dead on. That's when the idea flashed into my head. I didn't even want Ralph to continue reading. You see, over the summer I had started a story similar to this one but it was called something else and I hadn't thought about it for a while. By combining the two, I solved the problem Ralph had found and also made the story more descriptive and more exciting. Stealing from yourself is great! Now all I have to do is steal a better ending somewhere. Ralph says he saw the ending coming from about the second paragraph. Maybe it's time to switch readers!

Bill (age 12)

Personal response capitalizes on student diversity

The idea that whatever happens outside school hours has no bearing on the learning/teaching environment does not stand up. The opposite is true — everything has a bearing on students' ability to learn.

For this reason alone, in any classroom, the individual differences within the group are daunting. Even more daunting is the fact that individual students share a range of characteristics and that these characteristics shift and change in severity and importance according to the dictates of the lives they're leading.

Students appear in different sizes and shapes and vary in physical, social, emotional, and intellectual development. They come from diverse socio-economic backgrounds, from many countries and cultures, and operate in English as their first, second, or third language. Some are gregarious; some seldom speak.

Students belong to different sorts of families. Some come from one- and two-parent families; some are in foster homes, some in group homes. Some have a parent or guardian waiting for them when they arrive home from school; some are latch-key kids. Some have strong religious beliefs and some have no religion at all. One in ten is gay, lesbian, or bisexual.

Their intelligences vary. On standardized tests, including intelligence tests, some score very low and some very high, and most are strung out somewhere inbetween. Some show immediate aptitude for mathematical concepts; some have difficulty with simple arithmetic. Some still have difficulty reading in high school, while some have been reading fluently since before they started Kindergarten.

Their strengths and needs differ. Most are reasonably healthy; some are chronically ill. Some are admired athletes; some are scorned loners. Some are abused; some are enriched. Some have special gifts; some have special needs. Some thrive in the school environment; some fail day after day.

Students are nourished and nurtured in a variety of ways. Most had breakfast this morning; some didn't. Some were hugged before they came to school; some were beaten. They all laugh, at times, and some often cry. Some readily share their joy and grief, pleasure and pain, their frivolous enthusiasms, and their terrible secrets; some keep everything locked up inside.

All live intimate, intensely felt lives in which social concerns and pressures are paramount.

Curriculum should be pliable and flexible enough to meet the needs of these varied clients. With this kind of affective, cognitive, and socio-economic diversity, a "one size fits all" curriculum just doesn't work.

Personal response *capitalizes* on diversity, allowing teachers to customize the learning experience. Just as each tiny mountain stream discovers its own idiosyncratic path to the river, so individual learners forge their own personal pathways to understanding.

The intense nature of personal reflection through writing holds the potential to propel the individual from discovery to discovery. Meaning is the focal point, intrinsically, and the form of the writing is forged from that perspective.

In this final response, a thirteen-year-old, barely two years out of English as a Second Language classes, wrote an unsolicited poem to express and define what her response journal meant to her. Once integrated into regular classes and introduced to response journals, she immediately discovered that personal response allowed her to take control of her own learning.

When she recognized how essential the response technique had become to her own well-being as a learner, she began to examine the theme in poetic form. The theme was so important to her that she returned to the poem over the course of the year, revising it significantly time and again to suit the ever-widening vision she was gaining of her own learning processes.

Notice how the student's confidence and sense of self-worth are tied to the process of response and reflection, even in the use of the appropriate personal pronoun. She clearly demonstrates that she is a capable, self-motivated thinker who understands the pivotal role language plays in learning.

The final words on personal response belong to this student.

This one is for one of my teachers.
She taught me how to express myself.
I can tell her things by heart
And she understands what I feel.

I can learn things by seeing her face.
Her brain remembers every word I say,
Every dot, every letter.
She whispers into my ears.
If something is good, she talks smoothly.

She taught me how to sing high, sing low.
She guides me.
Whether I'm happy or sad, I'll still talk to her.
I share my adventures all the time.
She shows me why I do things.
She teaches me every day.

She cares about me,
She loves me,
She knows how to read my mind.
You can only find her by your imagination.
I'll love her forever . . . my response journal.

Evelyn Y. (age 13)

109

Glossary

The definitions in this selected glossary reflect the meanings that are used in the text.

affective a term from psychology referring to emotional activity

at risk a descriptor applied to students with academic, emotional, or social difficulties or a combination of these serious enough to jeopardize acceptable progress in school

brainstorming generating a list of examples, ideas, or questions to illustrate, expand, or explore a central idea or topic (record all ideas; no evaluating of ideas during collecting; quantity of ideas is important; encourage students to expand on each other's ideas; "zany" ideas are welcome)

cognitive a term from psychology referring to intellectual activity

conferencing opportunities to discuss ideas and problems in pairs or small groups; conferences can be conducted in a variety of formats with and without the teacher

cooperative learning a variety of small-group instructional techniques focusing on peer collaboration

"cueing" response a guiding suggestion or hint that gives an individual a sense of the kinds of responses possible. The "cues" serve as examples or models. Individuals are encouraged to develop their own responses based on their own purposes for reading and their personal perspectives as independent readers.

curriculum at one time, a synonym for syllabus; the current definition reflects the complexity of learning; in effect, it refers to everything that happens in a school.

diagnostic evaluation an aspect of formative evaluation; becoming familiar with each student's interests, abilities, preferred learning style, and learning difficulties

diary (private) an in-class record of personal observations, random jottings, and a daily record of thoughts and feelings; shared only if the student agrees

drafting the recursive cycle of revising and editing written material

drama in education involves all students in the classroom in spontaneous, unscripted, unrehearsed activities; no audience is present.

drama as performance involves selected students or professional actors in a planned, scripted, and rehearsed presentation in front of an audience

editing checking, prior to a final copy, for errors in spelling, usage, and clarity of expression

evaluation determining progress toward and attainment of specific goals; assessing student progress and achievement and program effectiveness

exposition written material intended to explain, clarify, or define

fluency the ability to speak, write, or read aloud smoothly, easily, and with clear expression of ideas; with independent reading, it has come to mean reading with mechanical competency and mature understanding

formative evaluation the ongoing assessment of student progress aimed almost exclusively at assisting learning and at improving the educational experience; geared to an individual's needs and personal growth

hemisphericity the concept that the left and right hemispheres of the brain have different capacities and functions; educators commonly speak of right-and-left-brain dominance, believing, for example, that the left brain controls speech and most language functions, while the right brain controls visual and spatial skills; theorizing that children may possess a dominant hemisphere, many educators advocate identifying and teaching to that dominance.

integrated program a term used in three different ways: an integrated program can refer to a blend of all aspects of English reading, writing, listening, speaking, viewing, and valuing; also, an individualized program related to the personal growth, skills, and cultural needs of the individual student; as well, a program coordinated with other aspects of a student's program: art, music, science, etc.

learning log day-to-day written records of what is done in a particular subject area, what and how students are learning, and how they feel about what they're doing

learning through language also referred to as "language across the curriculum," an approach to the learning/teaching environment that recognizes that language is intrinsic to thinking and learning; among the basic principles is the realization that students need to "think aloud" in their own informal talk or style of writing in order to fully understand concepts; during the talking and writing processes, concepts are examined, analyzed, reformulated, and defined in a personal and individual manner.

literacy the ability to read and write; extended today to include the processing of information from all sources and systems, including electronic and microelectronic

literature writing of high quality and significance because of a successful integration of components such as style, organization, language, and theme

"making meaning" the recognition that the act of processing language involves more than the communicating or recording of experience; through language we tend to construct our sense of things by clarifying, discovering, assessing, reflecting on, resolving, and refining what we really think and feel about experience

metacognition the study of thought processes

media literacy analyzing and reflecting on the ways in which media events are formulated and how they function

personal reading reading self-selected materials; also, reading material that may be suggested by someone else but which is so interesting and stimulating that the student becomes independently engaged by the experience

personal response encouraging students to begin an explication of and reflection on material with their own idiosyncratic, immediate, and spontaneous impressions, reactions, and questions where and when they arise; includes the recognition that our listening, speaking, reading, writing, viewing, and thinking processes are directed toward "making meaning."

personal writing writing about self-selected issues and events arising from an individual's daily life or interests; also, any writing that involves a student to such an extent that he/she is independently motivated to complete the experience

readalouds any material read aloud, usually by the teacher; students of all ages should be read to regularly; readalouds should comprise both fiction and non-fiction and should be drawn from a variety of genres

reading as process the recognition that reading is an active, personal, and recursive process integral to an individual's ongoing investigation into experience and that the process requires the integration of listening, speaking, writing, viewing, and thinking with reading to be fully effective

reductionism the process by which complex data or phenomena are reduced to their simplest constituent elements

response journal a notebook, folder, or electronic file in which students record their personal reactions to, questions about, and reflections on what they read, view, listen to, and discuss in addition to how they actually go about reading, viewing, listening, and discussing

response theory the proposition that understanding best begins with students explicating and reflecting on text with their own idiosyncratic, immediate, and spontaneous impressions, reactions, and questions where and when they arise

revision manipulating text by substituting, adding, deleting, and reordering words, phrases, sections, and ideas

risk taking the internalized understanding that mistakes/approximations are good; the freedom to experiment, extend the known, or try something new without unduly worrying about failing or being wrong

role playing exploring the thoughts and feelings of another by behaving and responding as that person

summative evaluation usually employs comparative standards and judgments in order to make an overall decision (e.g., any assessment made and recorded for report card purposes)

whole language a learning/teaching approach that emphasizes the integration of language "threads" (i.e., listening, speaking, reading, writing, thinking) within the context of meaningful communication (e.g., a single writing task may engage a student in a range of discussion, composing, editing/revising, reading tasks); includes the idea of moving away from isolated, fragmented approaches such as a regular "grammar" period outside the context of the writing process

writing as process the recursive and blended elements of writing: pre-writing, writing, post-writing; includes writing for real audiences other than the teacher and for purposes other than summative evaluation

writing-in-role extending the ability to grapple with problems and issues from a number of different perspectives by role playing in written form

writing folder a folder or notebook organized to accommodate and facilitate the various stages in the writing process; sometimes used as a synonym for writing as process

writer's journal a source book for writing containing random jottings made at home or school; carried and maintained by choice

writer's workshop organizing the classroom writing program to reflect and facilitate the writing process; includes such components as maintaining a writing folder, collaboration among students for composing, revising, and editing, and regular student-teacher conferences; frequent sharing and publishing of student writing are important features.

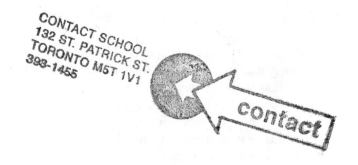

114

Index